Reader's Digest
Eggs, Milk
& Cheese

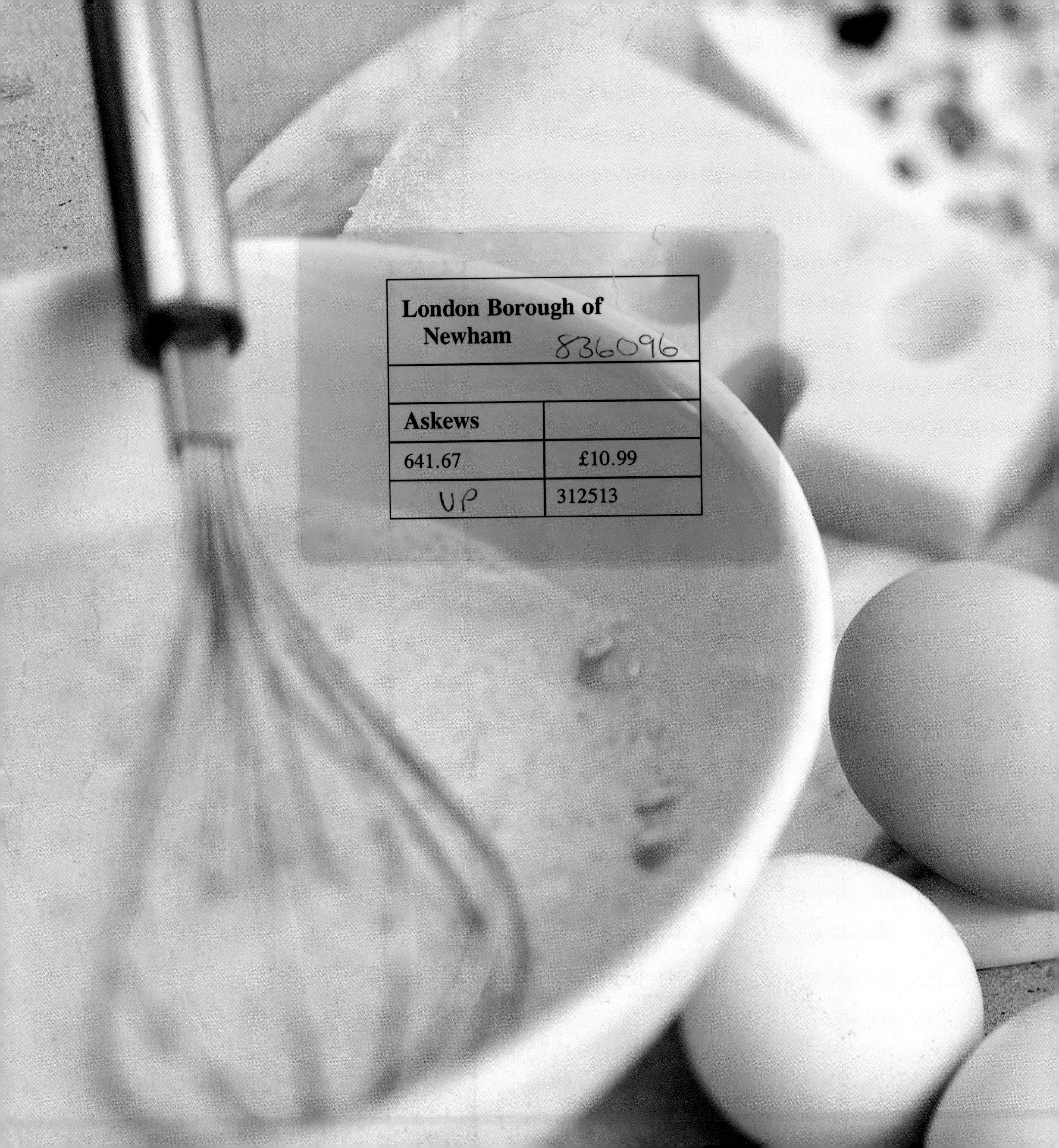

Reader's Digest
Eggs, Milk & Cheese

Published by The Reader's Digest Association Limited
London • New York • Sydney • Montreal

Eggs, Milk and Cheese is part of a series of cookery books called **Eat Well Live Well** and was created by Amazon Publishing Limited.

Series Editor *Norma MacMillan*
Volume Editors *Jane Middleton, Maggie Pannell*
Art Director *Ruth Prentice*
Photographic Direction *Ruth Prentice, Alison Shackleton*
DTP *Claire Graham*
Editorial Assistant *Elizabeth Woodland*
Nutritionist *Jane Griffin, BSc (Nutri.), SRD*

Contributors
Writers *Catherine Atkinson, Linda Collister, Christine France, Beverly LeBlanc, Jane Middleton, Angela Nilsen, Maggie Pannell, Anne Sheasby, Susanna Tee, Judith Wills*
Recipe Testers *Catherine Atkinson, Juliet Barker, Anna Brandenburger, Joanna Farrow, Maggie Pannell, Susanna Tee*
Photographers *Martin Brigdale, Gus Filgate, William Lingwood*
Stylist *Helen Trent*
Home Economists *Julz Beresford, Justine Kiggen, Lucy Miller, Bridget Sargeson, Linda Tubby, Sunil Vijayakar*

For Reader's Digest
Project Editor *Rachel Warren Chadd*
Project Art Editor *Louise Turpin*
Pre-press Accounts Manager *Penny Grose*

Reader's Digest General Books
Editorial Director *Cortina Butler*
Art Director *Nick Clark*
Series Editor *Christine Noble*

First Edition Copyright © 2002
The Reader's Digest Association Limited
11 Westferry Circus, Canary Wharf, London E14 4HE
www.readersdigest.co.uk

Paperback edition 2004
Paperback Art Editor *Jane McKenna*

ISBN 0 276 42890 0

Notes for the reader
• Use all metric or all imperial measures when preparing a recipe, as the two sets of measurements are not exact equivalents.
• Recipes were tested using metric measures and conventional (not fan-assisted) ovens. Medium eggs were used, unless otherwise specified.
• Can sizes are approximate, as weights can vary slightly according to the manufacturer.
• Preparation and cooking times are only intended as a guide.

The nutritional information in this book is for reference only. The editors urge anyone with continuing medical problems or symptoms to consult a doctor.

Contents

Eating well to live well

Eating a healthy diet can help you look good, feel great and have lots of energy. Nutrition fads come and go, but the simple keys to eating well remain the same: enjoy a variety of food – no single food contains all the vitamins, minerals, fibre and other essential components you need for health and vitality – and get the balance right by looking at the proportions of the different foods you eat. Add some regular exercise too – at least 30 minutes a day, 3 times a week – and you'll be helping yourself to live well and make the most of your true potential.

Getting it into proportion

Current guidelines are that most people in the UK should eat more starchy foods, more fruit and vegetables, and less fat, meat products and sugary foods. It is almost impossible to give exact amounts that you should eat, as every single person's requirements vary, depending on size, age and the amount of energy expended during the day. However, nutrition experts have suggested an ideal balance of the different foods that provide us with energy (calories) and the nutrients needed for health. The number of daily portions of each of the food groups will vary from person to person – for example, an active teenager might need to eat up to 14 portions of starchy carbohydrates every day, whereas a sedentary adult would only require 6 or 7 portions – but the proportions of the food groups in relation to each other should ideally stay the same.

More detailed explanations of food groups and nutritional terms can be found on pages 156–158, together with brief guidelines on amounts which can be used in conjunction with the nutritional analyses of the recipes. A simple way to get the balance right, however, is to imagine a daily 'plate' divided into the different food groups. On the imaginary 'plate', starchy carbohydrates fill at least one-third of the space, thus constituting the main part of your meals. Fruit and vegetables fill the same amount of space. The remaining third of the 'plate' is divided mainly between protein foods and dairy foods, with just a little space allowed for foods containing fat and sugar. These are the proportions to aim for.

It isn't essential to eat the ideal proportions on the 'plate' at every meal, or even every day – balancing them over a week or two is just as good. The healthiest diet for you and your family is one that is generally balanced and sustainable in the long term.

Our daily plate

Starchy carbohydrate foods: eat 6–14 portions a day
At least 50% of the calories in a healthy diet should come from carbohydrates, and most of that from starchy foods – bread, potatoes and other starchy vegetables, pasta, rice and cereals. For most people in the UK this means doubling current intake. Starchy carbohydrates are the best foods for energy. They also provide protein and essential vitamins and minerals, particularly those from the B group. Eat a variety of starchy foods, choosing wholemeal or wholegrain types whenever possible, because the fibre they contain helps to prevent constipation, bowel disease, heart disease and other health problems.

What is a portion of starchy foods?
Some examples are: 3 tbsp breakfast cereal • 2 tbsp muesli • 1 slice of bread or toast • 1 bread roll, bap or bun • 1 small pitta bread, naan bread or chapatti • 3 crackers or crispbreads • 1 medium-sized potato • 1 medium-sized plantain or small sweet potato • 2 heaped tbsp boiled rice • 2 heaped tbsp boiled pasta.

Fruit and vegetables: eat at least 5 portions a day
Nutrition experts are unanimous that we would all benefit from eating more fruit and vegetables each day – a total of at least 400 g (14 oz) of fruit and vegetables (edible part) is the target. Fruit and vegetables provide vitamin C for immunity and healing, and other 'antioxidant' vitamins and minerals for protection against cardiovascular disease and cancer. They also offer several 'phytochemicals' that help protect against cancer, and B vitamins, especially folate, which is important for women planning a pregnancy, to prevent birth defects. All of these, plus other nutrients, work together to boost well-being.

Antioxidant nutrients (e.g. vitamins C and beta-carotene, which are mainly derived from fruit and vegetables) and vitamin E help to prevent harmful free radicals in the body initiating or accelerating cancer, heart disease, cataracts, arthritis, general ageing, sun damage to skin, and damage to sperm. Free radicals occur naturally as a by-product of normal cell function, but are also caused by pollutants such as tobacco smoke and over-exposure to sunlight.

What is a portion of fruit or vegetables?
Some examples are: 1 medium-sized portion of vegetables or salad • 1 medium-sized piece of fresh fruit • 6 tbsp (about 140 g/5 oz) stewed or canned fruit • 1 small glass (100 ml/3½ fl oz) fruit juice.

Dairy foods: eat 2–3 portions a day
Dairy foods, such as milk, cheese, yogurt and fromage frais, are the best source of calcium for strong bones and teeth, and important for the nervous system. They also provide some protein for growth and repair, vitamin B_{12}, and vitamin A for healthy eyes. They are particularly valuable foods for young children, who need full-fat versions at least up to age 2. Dairy foods are also especially important for adolescent girls to prevent the development of osteoporosis later in life, and for women throughout life generally.

To limit fat intake, wherever possible adults should choose lower-fat dairy foods, such as semi-skimmed milk and low-fat yogurt.

What is a portion of dairy foods?
Some examples are: 1 medium-sized glass (200 ml/7 fl oz) milk • 1 matchbox-sized piece (40 g/1½ oz) Cheddar cheese • 1 small pot of yogurt • 125 g (4½ oz) cottage cheese or fromage frais.

Protein foods: eat 2–4 portions a day

Lean meat, fish, eggs and vegetarian alternatives provide protein for growth and cell repair, as well as iron to prevent anaemia. Meat also provides B vitamins for healthy nerves and digestion, especially vitamin B_{12}, and zinc for growth and healthy bones and skin. Only moderate amounts of these protein-rich foods are required. An adult woman needs about 45 g of protein a day and an adult man 55 g, which constitutes about 11% of a day's calories. This is less than the current average intake. For optimum health, we need to eat some protein every day.

What is a portion of protein-rich food?

Some examples are: 3 slices (85–100 g/3–3½ oz) of roast beef, pork, ham, lamb or chicken • about 100 g (3½ oz) grilled offal • 115–140 g (4–5 oz) cooked fillet of white or oily fish (not fried in batter) • 3 fish fingers • 2 eggs (up to 7 a week) • about 140 g/5 oz baked beans • 60 g (2¼ oz) nuts, peanut butter or other nut products.

Foods containing fat: 1–5 portions a day

Unlike fruit, vegetables and starchy carbohydrates, which can be eaten in abundance, fatty foods should not exceed 33% of the day's calories in a balanced diet, and only 10% of this should be from saturated fat. This quantity of fat may seem a lot, but it isn't – fat contains more than twice as many calories per gram as either carbohydrate or protein.

Overconsumption of fat is a major cause of weight and health problems. A healthy diet must contain a certain amount of fat to provide fat-soluble vitamins and essential fatty acids, needed for the development and function of the brain, eyes and nervous system, but we only need a small amount each day – just 25 g is required, which is much less than we consume in our Western diet. The current recommendations from the Department of Health are a maximum of 71 g fat (of this, 21.5 g saturated) for women each day and 93.5 g fat (28.5 g saturated) for men. The best sources of the essential fatty acids are natural fish oils and pure vegetable oils.

What is a portion of fatty foods?

Some examples are: 1 tsp butter or margarine • 2 tsp low-fat spread • 1 tsp cooking oil • 1 tbsp mayonnaise or vinaigrette (salad dressing) • 1 tbsp cream • 1 individual packet of crisps.

Foods containing sugar: 0–2 portions a day

Although many foods naturally contain sugars (e.g. fruit contains fructose, milk lactose), health experts recommend that we limit 'added' sugars. Added sugars, such as table sugar, provide only calories – they contain no vitamins, minerals or fibre to contribute to health, and it is not necessary to eat them at all. But, as the old adage goes, 'a little of what you fancy does you good' and sugar is no exception. Denial of foods, or using them as rewards or punishment, is not a healthy attitude to eating, and can lead to cravings, binges and yo-yo dieting. Sweet foods are a pleasurable part of a well-balanced diet, but added sugars should account for no more than 11% of the total daily carbohydrate intake.

In assessing how much sugar you consume, don't forget that it is a major ingredient of many processed and ready-prepared foods.

What is a portion of sugary foods?

Some examples are: 3 tsp sugar • 1 heaped tsp jam or honey • 2 biscuits • half a slice of cake • 1 doughnut • 1 Danish pastry • 1 small bar of chocolate • 1 small tube or bag of sweets.

Too salty

Salt (sodium chloride) is essential for a variety of body functions, but we tend to eat too much through consumption of salty processed foods, 'fast' foods and ready-prepared foods, and by adding salt in cooking and at the table. The end result can be rising blood pressure as we get older, which puts us at higher risk of heart disease and stroke. Eating more vegetables and fruit increases potassium intake, which can help to counteract the damaging effects of salt.

Alcohol in a healthy diet

In recent research, moderate drinking of alcohol has been linked with a reduced risk of heart disease and stroke among men and women over 45. However, because of other risks associated with alcohol, particularly in excessive quantities, no doctor would recommend taking up drinking if you are teetotal. The healthiest pattern of drinking is to enjoy small amounts of alcohol with food, to have alcohol-free days and always to avoid getting drunk. A well-balanced diet is vital because nutrients from food (vitamins and minerals) are needed to detoxify the alcohol.

Water – the best choice

Drinking plenty of non-alcoholic liquid each day is an often overlooked part of a well-balanced diet. A minimum of 8 glasses (which is about 2 litres/3½ pints) is the ideal. If possible, these should not all be tea or coffee, as these are stimulants and diuretics, which cause the body to lose liquids, taking with them water-soluble vitamins. Water is the best choice. Other good choices are fruit or herb teas or tisanes, fruit juices – diluted with water, if preferred – or semi-skimmed milk (full-fat milk for very young children). Fizzy sugary or acidic drinks such as cola are more likely to damage tooth enamel than other drinks.

As a guide to the vitamin and mineral content of foods and recipes in the book, we have used the following terms and symbols, based on the percentage of the daily RNI provided by one serving for the average adult man or woman aged 19–49 years (see also pages 156–158):

✓✓✓ *or* excellent   at least 50% (half)

✓✓   *or* good   25–50% (one-quarter to one-half)

✓   *or* useful   10–25% (one-tenth to one-quarter)

Note that recipes contribute other nutrients, but the analyses only include those that provide at least 10% RNI per portion. Vitamins and minerals where deficiencies are rare are not included.

Ⓥ denotes that a recipe is suitable for vegetarians.

Fresh Eggs and Dairy Foods

Natural produce – foods full of goodness

Milk has been enjoyed as a nutritious food for thousands of years, not only as a high-vitality drink but also in the myriad cheese, yogurt, cream and butter products made from it. Supplying protein and many vitamins and minerals – in particular calcium – milk and other dairy products can play a vital part in maintaining good health for everyone in the family. Eggs, too, are an important food to include in a healthy, well-balanced diet, providing high-quality protein and plenty of other beneficial nutrients – and all in a very convenient little package.

Healthy eggs, milk and cheese

Eggs and dairy products are rich in a wide range of nutrients, including high-quality protein, many vitamins, and essential minerals such as calcium. When eaten as part of a varied and well-balanced diet, they can make an important contribution to good health. Mixing well with other ingredients, they are also endlessly versatile.

Why eat eggs, milk and cheese?

Since animals were first domesticated thousands of years ago, we have used their eggs and milk as food. Today, hen's eggs and cow's milk are the most common, but we can also enjoy duck, quail and goose eggs, as well as dairy products – such as cream, yogurt, butter and cheese – made from the milk of sheep, goats and water buffalo.

Most of us use eggs and some form of dairy products in the kitchen every day, and these staple foods have a lot to offer nutritionally.

● Eggs and dairy products, apart from cream, provide high-quality protein – protein that contains all 8 of the essential amino acids. A regular intake of protein is needed for optimum health.

● Eggs are a useful source of vitamins A, B_{12}, E and niacin, as well as providing zinc, potassium, magnesium, calcium, selenium and iodine. They also contain iron, although it is not in a form that is easily absorbed by the body.

● Dairy products provide conjugated linoleic acid, which may help to protect against heart attacks.

● Milk, yogurt and cheese are rich in calcium, phosphorus and B vitamins, especially B_2 and B_{12}. They also contain some zinc and magnesium.

● Full-fat milk, cream and many cheeses are a valuable source of vitamin A.

● Yogurt offers excellent amounts of potassium and iodine.

Calcium throughout life

One of the key reasons for including dairy products in the diet is that they are rich in calcium. Although this vital mineral is available in some other foods, such as dark leafy greens, nuts and seeds, it appears in the greatest quantities and in the most readily assimilated form in dairy products. As long as there is an adequate intake of vitamin D (from eggs and oily fish as well as the action of sunlight on skin), the body can take full advantage of the calcium on offer.

● Children and teenagers need plenty of calcium to maintain optimum bone and tooth development, while pregnant and breastfeeding women need calcium to perform the same task for their baby.

● Young adults should ensure a good supply of calcium to help build 'peak bone mass', which is reached at around the age of 30. The larger and stronger the bones, the more able they will be to cope with bone demineralisation in later life.

● Adults, particularly women, need calcium to help maintain optimum bone density throughout life, which in turn will help to minimise the effects of osteoporosis after the menopause.

● High-calcium dairy products are good for oral health. In a recent study, people who regularly ate at least 3 portions of dairy products a day had a 50% reduction in the risk of gum

When you need a little extra …

There are certain times in our lives when we have special dietary needs, and eating eggs and a good variety of dairy products is an excellent way to meet these extra requirements.

● Small children need extra calcium to help the growth of healthy bones and teeth.

● From the ages of 15–18, teenagers need around 10% more calories than adults.

● Pregnant and breastfeeding women need extra calcium and vitamins A, B and D. Women need to increase their daily calorie intake by about 200 kcal during the last 3 months of pregnancy and by about 500 kcal while breastfeeding.

▲ For a special breakfast or brunch, dip brioche into egg and milk, fry until golden brown and serve with raspberries, sliced peaches and Greek-style yogurt (see Another idea, page 36)

▲ Toss a Puy lentil and rice salad with a chilli dressing and top with griddled slices of halloumi cheese (see Some more ideas, page 63)

▼ Layer a fresh plum purée with a creamy mixture of fromage frais and bio yogurt for a delectable dessert (see Some more ideas, page 140)

disease and tooth decay. And it has been shown that eating cheese after a meal helps to protect against dental erosion.

Minerals are principally found in the non-fat part of milk, so semi-skimmed and skimmed milk contain more calcium than full-fat varieties.

Disproving the bad press

In recent years our consumption of eggs and dairy products has declined, mainly because they are perceived to be high in cholesterol and saturated fat. In fact, this reputation is largely undeserved. For example, for most people, eating foods that contain cholesterol, as eggs do, will not have an adverse effect on blood cholesterol levels and so does not increase the risk of heart disease. With regard to fat in dairy products, many have a medium or low fat content. And with all the positive benefits of dairy products, even higher-fat items such as hard cheeses are well worth including in a healthy diet.

Nutritious and versatile eggs

It has long been known that eggs are one of the most valuable foods in the cook's repertoire. Not only are they excellent prepared quite simply – poached, scrambled and so on – but they are indispensable in a wide range of recipes. And they have a lot of health benefits to offer as well as being one of the cheapest sources of protein.

The goodness of eggs

Eggs are designed by nature to be a complete food package for the growing chick. This means they contain a wide range of essential nutrients, including protein (12.5 g per 100 g/ 3½ oz), plenty of minerals, such as calcium, iodine, iron, magnesium, potassium, zinc and selenium, and vitamins A, D, E and many from the B group. Eggs are not high in fat, and almost two-thirds of the fat present is unsaturated – 47% of it monounsaturated and 12% polyunsaturated.

A small hen's egg, weighing about 50 g (scant 2 oz), contains 75 kcal, a medium egg 85–90 kcal and a large egg about 100 kcal. Most of the calories, fat and nutrients – and all of the cholesterol – are in the yolk. The white (albumen) is 88% water, with the rest mostly protein, plus a good amount of potassium and vitamin B_2.

The cholesterol question

Too much cholesterol in the blood can increase the risk of coronary heart disease, and because of this some people have had reservations about eating eggs – eggs are fairly high in dietary cholesterol, with about 217 mg in a medium egg. However, it is now recognised that the amount of fat you eat, particularly saturated or trans fats, will have more effect on blood cholesterol levels than cholesterol intake through food. The current advice is that people in normal health can eat up to 7 eggs a week. (People being treated for high blood lipids and cholesterol may receive different advice and should consult their doctor, dietician or nutritionist.)

Brown, white, pale blue, green, pink ...

Most hen's eggs are brown or white, although there are other colours appearing in supermarkets now. The colour of the shell makes no difference to the nutritional or cooking quality of the egg – it is purely a reflection of the breed of hen. The colour of the yolk, too, may vary from egg to egg, and largely depends on the hen's diet. For example, a deep yellow yolk can be an indication of an egg from an organic or free-range hen that has been fed on maize. However, the feed for battery hens is sometimes adulterated with artificial colourings to give the yolks a similar deep yellow colour.

Types of egg

Although the majority of eggs consumed are hen's, we can also eat eggs from other birds such as ducks, geese and quails. **Bantam's eggs** are small and tasty, and usually have a white shell. Bantams are a smaller variety of hen.

bantam's eggs

duck eggs

goose eggs

Egg safety

Salmonella bacteria, which can cause food poisoning, are present in some eggs. The bacteria are destroyed when eggs are thoroughly cooked – for example, during hard-boiling. However, if eggs are used raw, such as in home-made mayonnaise, or only lightly cooked, such as soft-boiled, poached and lightly scrambled eggs, there is a risk of salmonella poisoning. The Department of Health recommends that everyone avoid raw eggs, and that vulnerable groups such as pregnant women, young children, the very old, the ill and people with damaged immune systems avoid eating lightly cooked eggs.

Duck eggs are much larger than hen's eggs and have a stronger flavour. They are slightly higher in fat, protein and cholesterol, and are also higher in iron and vitamins A, B group and D. Duck eggs can generally be used in cooking in the same ways as hen's eggs, although the strong flavour should be borne in mind. For safety, however, it is best not to use them in recipes that require lightly cooked eggs – they should be boiled for at least 10 minutes. Unless otherwise stated on the box, they are likely to come from intensively reared ducks.

Goose eggs are the largest of all the eggs you are likely to find on sale. They have a similar flavour and nutritional profile to hen's eggs, and can be used in all hen's egg recipes and basic dishes. They are likely to be free range.

Hen's eggs are graded according to size – small, medium, large and extra large or very large. About 90% of commercial eggs come from battery-reared hens. Barn eggs come from hens that are still very intensively farmed but are not confined to cages. Free-range hens are allowed more space and some outdoor living, although conditions can vary widely. Organic eggs come from hens that are reared according to strict dietary stipulations. Labels such as 'farm fresh' and 'country' hint at a natural upbringing for the hen but are entirely meaningless – usually these eggs come from battery hens.

Quail's eggs are tiny, with pretty speckled shells and a delicate flavour. Almost all quail's eggs sold are from battery-farmed birds. They have a similar nutritional composition to hen's eggs, with 6 quail's eggs being roughly equivalent to 1 hen's egg. Use them in the same way as hen's eggs, bearing in mind that because of their size cooking times will be shorter.

Egg storage

Eggs should be stored in the fridge, and it is best to leave them in their box so you can keep an eye on the date stamp, using older eggs first. They can usually be kept for up to 3 weeks. Don't store them next to strong-smelling foods – as their shells are porous they easily pick up odours and even flavours. They should also be kept away from possible contaminants such as raw meat and poultry.

Checking eggs for freshness

Most egg boxes are marked with a packing date rather than a laying date, so it is important to bear in mind that the eggs may have been several days old when they were packed. For an indication of the egg's age, look at the 'best before' date: on those with the Lion stamp, this will be 3 weeks after the egg was laid. This 21-day standard is not a legal requisite, so on other non-Lion-stamped eggs the best before date could be up to 28 days from laying.

When a fresh egg is cracked open, it will have a round, plump yolk and a thick white that clings closely to the yolk, with a thinner outer layer that spreads out around the inner white only a short way. The older the egg, the flatter the yolk and the flatter, thinner and runnier the white will be. Eggs that have gone bad have an unmistakable sulphurous smell.

To check if a raw egg in its shell is fresh, immerse it in a glass of cold water: if it lies horizontally at the bottom it is very fresh; if it begins to point upwards it is about a week old; if it stands vertically it is stale. A fresh egg tends to feel heavy in the hand, because the older the egg, the more water inside it will have evaporated.

hen's eggs

quail's eggs

Cooking eggs

It's hard to imagine a more versatile ingredient than the egg. It forms the basis for pancakes and other batters, helps to set savoury and sweet tarts, and enriches and flavours most cakes and many desserts. Egg yolks are indispensable for thickening sauces, and whisked egg whites add volume and lightness to soufflés and many other dishes.

In some cases, the age of an egg may affect the success of a dish. Very fresh eggs give the best results when poaching and frying, and are also a better choice for soft-boiling, omelettes, scrambling and general cooking. However, very fresh eggs (only a few days old) are not ideal for hard-boiling, as the shell and the membrane just underneath it will be hard to peel off. Eggs 1–2 weeks old are the best for hard-boiling.

Once you have mastered these basic cooking methods, you will have the foundation for a wide range of meals at your fingertips. Timings given are for hen's eggs.

Boiling

Put a medium egg (at room temperature) into a saucepan with tepid water to cover. Bring to the boil, then reduce the heat and simmer for 3–4 minutes for soft-boiled and 7 minutes for hard-boiled. Large eggs will take 4–5 minutes for soft-boiled and 8 minutes for hard-boiled.

Remove the egg with a slotted spoon. If soft-boiled, remove the 'cap' or top of the shell straightaway, to arrest the cooking process. Place hard-boiled eggs in a bowl of cold water to cool (this helps to prevent a black ring forming around the yolk), then peel them when cool enough to handle.

Poaching

Bring a frying pan of water at least 4 cm (1½ in) deep to a simmer. If you like, add 1 tsp vinegar to the water to help speed the coagulation of the albumen and thus preserve the shape of the egg (you will not need the vinegar if your eggs are very fresh). Carefully break the eggs into the water one at a time (or break each one into a cup and slide it into the water). Poach for about 3 minutes, by which time the whites should be set and the yolks still a bit runny (poach for another minute if you prefer the yolk to be set). Towards the end of the cooking, baste the yolks with the simmering water. Lift out each egg with a draining spoon and, with the egg still on the

spoon, rest it on some kitchen paper for a few seconds to absorb any water. If you like, trim the edges of the egg with kitchen scissors to neaten any straggly bits of white, then serve. Poached eggs can be kept in the fridge for a day and reheated for 1 minute in hot water.

Scrambling

Break the eggs into a bowl and add 1 tbsp semi-skimmed milk per egg, plus salt and pepper to taste. Whisk thoroughly to combine. Heat a small knob of butter in a non-stick saucepan over a moderate heat. When it has melted, pour in the egg mixture and cook, stirring frequently, until the eggs are almost set but are still soft and glossy looking. Remove from the heat, as the eggs will continue to cook in the heat of the pan – take care not to overcook or the eggs will become dry and grainy.

Scrambled eggs can also be cooked in a double saucepan or heatproof bowl set over a pan of hot water.

Baking (en cocotte)

Lightly oil or butter 7.5 cm (3 in) ramekin dishes and break an egg into each one. (For a more substantial dish, put a little smoked fish or lightly cooked spinach or mushrooms in the ramekins first.) Season and top with a small knob of butter. Set the dishes in a baking tin and pour enough boiling water into the tin to come halfway up the sides of the ramekins. Bake in a preheated 180°C (350°F, gas mark 4) oven for 10–15 minutes or until set. Serve hot.

Frying

Melt a small knob of butter in a non-stick frying pan over a moderate heat. Break the eggs into the pan, then reduce the heat a little and cover the pan. Fry for 4–6 minutes or until the eggs are cooked to your taste. Alternatively, do not cover the pan and instead, when the whites are set, carefully flip the eggs over using a fish slice. Fry for about 30 seconds longer.

Making a folded French omelette

Whisk 2 eggs in a bowl with 1 tbsp cold water and seasoning to taste. Melt a small knob of butter in a 15–18 cm (6–7 in) non-stick omelette or frying pan over a high heat, swirling it around as it melts. When the butter is foaming, add the egg mixture. After a few seconds, tilt the pan and use a spatula to

scrambling

boiling

frying

baking
en cocotte

folding an omelette

poaching

draw the cooked egg into the centre, so that the uncooked egg can run onto the pan. Continue tilting the pan and drawing the cooked egg in, to build up a plump omelette. When there is very little runny egg left, add any filling, such as grated cheese, diced tomatoes, cooked vegetables and so on, then leave the omelette undisturbed for about 10 seconds so that it can set and become golden on the base. Remove from the heat and use the spatula to fold one-third of the omelette over towards the centre. Slide the omelette across the pan and roll it onto a serving plate (the folds should be underneath as the omelette lands on the plate).

To make a soufflé omelette, separate the eggs and beat the yolks with seasoning to taste. In a separate bowl, whisk the whites until stiff, then fold them into the yolks. Cook in the butter until set and golden on the base, without moving the egg mixture in the pan, then transfer to a preheated grill to finish cooking and set the top.

Fresh foods from the dairy

Milk is a staple in most kitchens, and offers many valuable nutrients in an easy-to-enjoy form. It also provides the basis for butter and cream, two of life's little luxuries. Because of their high fat content, butter and cream should be used with more discretion, but they too can contribute good things to our diet.

Milk

The many different types of milk available to us today are in sharp contrast to what the milkman brought 50 or so years ago. We can now choose to drink cow's milk, or that of other animals, such as goats, sheep or even water buffalo, and we can opt for lower-fat versions.

All fresh milk should be kept, covered, in the fridge and used by the date on the lid or carton. Exposure to sunlight destroys vitamin B_2, so bottles of milk should not be left on the doorstep all day. Cow's milk and goat's milk freeze well in their cartons or in freezer containers; they can be kept for up to 1 month.

Breakfast milk, sometimes labelled Channel Island milk, comes from Jersey and Guernsey cows and is richer in fat than ordinary full-fat milk.

Condensed milk, available in both full-fat and skimmed versions, is made by heating milk to remove some of the water content and then adding sugar to act as a preservative. The thick, heavily sweetened milk, which will keep for several months, has a toffee-like taste.

Dried milk is made by evaporating skimmed milk. The resulting powder can be stored for several months, and is simply mixed with water to reconstitute it. Since the advent of UHT milk, this method of keeping milk long term is not used so much.

Evaporated milk is a concentrated version of full-fat or skimmed milk that has been heated to remove much of its water content, and then sterilised so that it will keep well. It is slightly darker than fresh milk and has a 'cooked' flavour.

Full-fat milk, or whole milk, is milk from the cow with nothing added and nothing taken away. It retains all of the fat-soluble vitamins that are lost from semi-skimmed and skimmed milk, although it is slightly lower in calcium than they are. Children should be given full-fat milk after the age of 1 year, although semi-skimmed milk can be introduced gradually after the age of 2, and skimmed milk usually after the age of 5, if the child's nutrient intake is otherwise adequate and growth is satisfactory.

Goat's milk, available in full-fat, skimmed and long-life versions, is slightly creamier than cow's milk but has a similar taste. Some people find it easier to digest than cow's milk.

Nutritional content of milk and cream per 100 ml (3½ fl oz)

	kcal	fat (g)	protein (g)	calcium (mg)
Milk				
breakfast	78	4.8	3.6	130
condensed (full-fat)	333	10.1	8.5	330
evaporated (full-fat)	151	9.4	8.4	290
full-fat	66	3.9	3.2	115
goat's (full-fat)	60	3.5	3.1	100
semi-skimmed	46	1.8	3.3	120
sheep's	95	6.0	5.4	170
skimmed	33	0.1–0.3	3.3	120
Cream				
clotted	586	63	1.6	37
crème fraîche	380	40	2.4	50
double	449	48	1.7	50
single	198	19	2.6	91
soured	205	20	2.9	93
whipping	373	39	2.0	62

semi-skimmed milk
skimmed milk
skimmed condensed milk
goat's milk
full-fat condensed milk
full-fat milk
UHT milk
breakfast milk
dried milk
homogenised milk
evaporated milk
sheep's milk

Homogenised milk has been treated to distribute the fat evenly. If full-fat milk is not homogenised, it will separate into layers, with the cream on top and semi-skimmed milk underneath.

Pasteurised milk has been flash-heated for 5 seconds to destroy most of the bacteria naturally present and to improve its keeping qualities. Almost all of the milk sold in the UK is pasteurised. Most of the vitamin content is retained, although some beneficial bacteria are lost.

Semi-skimmed milk has had about half of its fat removed, taking more than half the fat-soluble vitamins with it but leaving the calcium and protein. It is a good compromise for people who prefer a slightly richer taste than skimmed milk but who find full-fat milk too creamy.

Sheep's milk, which is usually higher in fat than goat's milk, may also be suitable for people who find cow's milk difficult to digest. However, it is not widely available.

Skimmed milk has had almost all of the fat removed, giving it a rather thin, watery consistency. It has lost the fat-soluble vitamins A, D and E, but retains most of its other nutrients, such as calcium and protein.

UHT (ultra-heat-treated) milk has been pasteurised and then subjected to heat to kill off any bacteria present – a process that may also reduce the vitamin B content, although it does not affect the flavour. A carton of UHT milk can be kept at room temperature for up to 6 months, but once opened it should be stored in the fridge like fresh milk.

Lactose intolerance

A high proportion of the world's population is not able to digest the lactose (milk sugars) in milk because of a deficiency in the enzyme lactase – this enzyme breaks down the lactose in the digestive system. The undigested lactose remains in the gut, where it can cause long-term health problems. Avoiding lactose is the usual answer for such people. Lactose is found in the milk and milk byproducts of cows, goats and sheep. Some people with lactose intolerance find they can tolerate goat's and sheep's milk better than cow's milk. Acidophilus milk, which is pasteurised cow's milk to which *Lactobacillus* bacteria have been reintroduced, is easier to digest than ordinary cow's milk, and may provide another alternative. Some cheeses, including Brie, Edam and pecorino, contain only very small amounts of lactose and may therefore be tolerated. If you think you may be lactose-intolerant, seek advice from your doctor before making any changes to your diet.

Cream

Cream is the fat that rises to the surface of fresh milk and is skimmed off. Generally, the thicker the cream, the higher the fat content. All the different types contain useful amounts of vitamin A, calcium and phosphorus.

Fresh cream should be kept, covered, in the fridge and used by the date on the carton.

Clotted cream, traditionally made in the West Country, is the thickest and richest of the dairy creams. Its pale yellow colour and thick texture are obtained by heating full-fat milk to evaporate some of the liquid and then skimming off the creamy crust. Clotted cream is usually served as an accompaniment to desserts and to top scones rather than used in cooking.

Crème fraîche, originally from Normandy in France, has a similar taste to soured cream but is less acidic. Because it is treated with a lactic culture it is very thick, although surprisingly its fat content is lower than that of double cream. Crème fraîche keeps well and is a good all-round cooking cream, as it never separates when boiled. A half-fat version is available, which often includes thickeners and other additives.

Double cream is high in fat, so is best used sparingly. As it can be boiled, it is added to sweet and savoury sauces to enrich them. It can also be whipped to a soft or firm consistency.

Single cream cannot be whipped, but is good for pouring or for using in cooking when you want a richer texture or flavour than milk will give. Extra-thick single cream has a similar texture to very lightly whipped double cream.

Smetana is similar to soured cream but is made from single cream and skimmed milk, and is therefore lower in fat than soured cream.

Soured cream is fresh single cream that has been soured and slightly thickened by the addition of lactic acid-producing bacteria, giving it a tangy flavour. The souring also makes it easier to digest than single cream.

Whipping cream is slightly less rich than double cream and is quicker and easier to whip, with a consistent, light result. It can be mixed with lower-fat dairy products such as plain yogurt to make a rich-tasting but lower-calorie alternative to whipped cream.

Butter

Butter is made by churning cream. It is a good source of the fat-soluble vitamins A and D, and it contains 15 mg calcium per 100 g (3½ oz). It is also high in saturated fat, at 67% of its total fat content, and in calories (727 kcal per 100 g/3½ oz). Half-fat butter, which contains half the fat and calories of standard butter, is available; it is not suitable for baking.

Several studies show that the natural fats in butter do not have an adverse effect on blood cholesterol levels in the same way as the artificial trans fats in many commercial hydrogenated margarines and low-fat spreads. So a little butter eaten within an overall healthy diet is not such a bad thing, and there is nothing to compare with the flavour it brings.

● Buy good-quality butter – its taste, colour and texture will be superior. The cream used to make French butter has often been treated with a lactic culture, which gives it more flavour.

● Salt improves the keeping qualities of butter in the fridge.

● Butter should be stored in a lidded butter dish or in its own wrapping in the fridge. If kept out at room temperature it will soon go 'off' and taste rancid, and must be discarded.

● Butter freezes well. Salted butter can be kept for 3 months, and unsalted butter for 6 months.

● For spreading, let butter come to room temperature, or try special 'spreadable' butter that can be used straight from the fridge. If the butter is soft, you'll spread less of it on bread.

● Butter burns at high temperatures so it is generally not used on its own for frying. Instead, it is best mixed with oil.

Milk and egg sauces

These simple sauces form the basis for many other dishes or are served alongside. If you dress them up with flavourings – cheese and herbs in the basic white sauce, orange zest or liqueur in the custard, for example – they can really make an impact and turn a meal into something special.

Basic white sauce

Makes about 600 ml (1 pint), to serve 4

55 g (2 oz) butter
55 g (2 oz) plain flour
600 ml (1 pint) semi-skimmed milk
salt and pepper

Preparation time: 5 minutes
Cooking time: 5 minutes

1 Melt the butter in a heavy-based saucepan over a low heat. Remove from the heat and stir in the flour. Gradually pour in the milk, stirring or whisking constantly.
2 Return the pan to the heat and bring to the boil, still stirring or whisking. Reduce the heat and simmer the sauce gently for 5 minutes, stirring occasionally. Taste and season with salt and pepper. Serve or use immediately.

Another idea

● For a low-fat cornflour-thickened white sauce, omit the butter and flour, and instead mix 4 tbsp cornflour to a smooth paste with a little of the milk. Heat the remaining milk to boiling point, then pour a little of it onto the cornflour mixture, stirring. Return this to the milk in the saucepan. Bring to the boil, stirring, until the sauce thickens, then simmer for 3 minutes. This makes a thick sauce; for a thinner one, use 3 tbsp cornflour.

Custard

Makes about 600 ml (1 pint), to serve 4

4 egg yolks
4 tsp cornflour
4 tbsp caster sugar
600 ml (1 pint) semi-skimmed milk

Preparation time: 5 minutes
Cooking time: 5 minutes

1 Put the egg yolks, cornflour and sugar in a bowl and beat until smooth.
2 Pour the milk into a saucepan and bring to the boil, then slowly pour it onto the egg yolk mixture, stirring thoroughly.
3 Return the mixture to the saucepan and cook over a low heat, stirring constantly, until it thickens to a custard consistency. It should reach 82°C (180°F) on a cooking thermometer. Remove from the heat and strain into a bowl. Serve hot or leave to cool before using or serving.

Culturing milk into yogurt

Yogurt has many health benefits to offer, being rich in nutrients and containing bacteria that are helpful to the digestive and immune systems. There are many different varieties of yogurt available now, from rich and creamy to lower-fat versions, so it is easy to include this useful and delicious dairy food in the diet.

The benefits of yogurt

Yogurt is a thick, creamy, slightly acidic-tasting dairy product, made by curdling (or fermenting) warmed pasteurised milk with lactic acid cultures (bacteria). It is easily digested and some people can tolerate it better than milk. The nutritional profile of yogurt varies according to what type of milk it is made from, how it is produced and what is added to it, but generally it is a good source of protein, B vitamins and calcium, and is low or fairly low in fat.

Most yogurts on sale are 'live' (although this is not always stated on the label), which means they contain living bacteria that are beneficial to the digestive system – usually *Lactobacillus bulgaricus* and *Streptococcus thermophilus*. Bio yogurt contains a slightly different bacterial culture, aimed specifically at redressing the natural balance of the gut flora.

There is evidence that if the gut is colonised sufficiently with friendly bacteria, there may be an improvement in conditions such as candida and in stomach upsets such as diarrhoea and flatulence. They may also help to prevent problems such as cow's milk allergy and eczema in infants, and help to strengthen the immune system. Eating plenty of yogurt is sometimes recommended after a course of antibiotics, which can reduce the amount of beneficial bacteria in the gut.

Yogurt should be stored, covered, in the fridge. Unopened, it will keep until its 'use-by' date; once opened it should be used within 1–2 days. It is not suitable for freezing.

If yogurt is to be added to a dish that is cooked over a high heat, it needs to be stabilised first with a little cornflour, to prevent it from separating.

Types of yogurt

Most of the different kinds of yogurt are available both plain (or natural) and flavoured. Many flavoured yogurts contain artificial sweeteners or sugar, flavourings and colourings, plus gelatine and other thickeners. The best contain only plain yogurt plus natural flavourings such as fruit purées.

Full-fat or whole-milk yogurt is rich and creamy. It can be used as a lower-fat alternative to cream in many dishes, adding a delightful piquant taste.

Goat's milk yogurt, which is becoming more widely available, has a pleasant, mild taste. It may be suitable for people who cannot eat cow's milk products. Low-fat, full-fat and bio versions are produced.

Greek-style yogurt is traditionally made from full-fat sheep's milk, though cow's milk versions are also available. It is strained to remove some of the liquid, making it very thick and rich, with a delicious creamy flavour – and a higher fat content than other yogurts. A 0% fat version is also available. Greek-style yogurt makes an excellent alternative to whipped cream as a topping for desserts. It can also be used in cooking.

Nutritional content of different yogurts per 100 g (3½ oz)

	kcal	fat (g)	protein (g)	calcium (mg)
full-fat	79	3	5	200
goat's milk, bio	105	7.3	5.5	159
Greek-style	115	9	6	150
low-fat plain	56	less than 1	5	190
sheep's milk	106	7.5	4.4	150

Low-fat yogurt, made from skimmed milk, is available in 'set' (firm) or 'stirred' (runny) versions. Bio low-fat yogurt tends to taste milder and creamier than non-bio varieties. Plain low-fat yogurt is a delicious ingredient for hot and cold dishes.
Sheep's milk yogurt, other than traditional Greek varieties, is not widely available.

Other cultured milk products

Cultured milk products are becoming increasingly popular as their nutritional benefits are recognised.

'Bio' milks are flavoured, sweetened milks to which the *Lactobacillus* bacteria have been added. They have similar health benefits to live yogurt.
Buttermilk is traditionally a byproduct of making butter – the whey left after churning. Nowadays, most buttermilk available in the shops is made by adding cultures to skimmed milk. It is low in calories and fat (37 kcal and less than 1 g fat per 100 ml/3½ fl oz) and, with its slightly acidic quality, is ideal for making scones and soda bread. It also makes a refreshing, easily digested drink.

Making yogurt

You can buy electric yogurt makers, either with 6 or 8 small pots or 1 large pot. These are simple and convenient to use, but it is also very easy to make yogurt without any special equipment. All you need is a little plain live yogurt and some milk – skimmed, semi-skimmed or full-fat, depending on how rich you want your yogurt to be. Use at least 600 ml (1 pint) milk – it is not really worth going to the trouble of making less yogurt than this.

● Bring the milk to the boil, then leave it to cool to blood heat, which is around 37°C (98°F) – a thermometer will help here.

● Stir 1 tbsp plain live yogurt into the milk, then pour it into a bowl or wide-necked flask. Cover and leave in a warm place such as an airing cupboard for 8–12 hours, by which time it will have set. Transfer to the fridge.

● Home-made yogurt can be used plain or you can flavour it as desired, with fresh fruit, fruit purée, honey, chopped nuts or a few drops of pure vanilla extract.

● To make Greek-style yogurt, once your yogurt has set put it into a large muslin bag, or a sieve lined with muslin, and suspend it over a bowl. Put it into the fridge. The liquid will drip through into the bowl, leaving you with firmer, thicker yogurt. The longer you let it drain, the more like a soft, fresh cheese it will become. Discard the liquid in the bowl, or use it in cooking as a tangy substitute for milk.

▲ A thermometer – here one suitable for taking people's temperatures – is an accurate way to check if the milk is at blood heat

▲ You can use bought or previously home-made yogurt as the 'starter' culture

▲ Adding fresh fruit to home-made yogurt will boost its vitamin and antioxidant content

▲ Draining the yogurt in a sieve lined with muslin will make it thick and creamy

fresh eggs and dairy foods

Cheese variety

Whether eaten simply with bread for lunch or as the finale to a many-course menu, whether melted or baked, or whipped up into a soufflé or spread, cheese is deliciously satisfying and nutritious. It comes in an infinite variety of forms, flavours and textures, yet all cheeses start with the same product – milk.

How cheese is made

Cheese is most commonly made from cow's milk, but goat's, sheep's and water buffalo milk are also used – and even the milk of reindeer, asses, mares and camels in some parts of the world. The simplest forms of cheese are made by coagulating, or curdling, the milk. This can happen naturally – warm milk left out long enough becomes sour and then curdles into whitish lumps (curds) in a thin liquid called whey, which is drained off. However, for commercial production a bacterial culture or starter is usually added to sour the milk, and rennet is used to aid the curdling.

Traditionally, rennet is a substance obtained from the stomach lining of young calves. However, nowadays many cheeses are produced with a vegetarian microbial starter or a genetically engineered rennet, both of which are suitable for a vegetarian diet.

The curds are sometimes heated or scalded and, in the case of hard cheeses, pressed to remove more whey. Then they are moulded or shaped, salted and left to ripen or mature under controlled conditions. The ripening or maturing process may take anywhere from several weeks to years, depending upon the cheese-maker and the type of cheese.

Cheese in a healthy diet

Since most cheeses are a concentrated food, they are a particularly rich source of the nutrients they offer. So just a little can have a big impact on the vitamins, minerals and protein in a meal.

In general, the harder the cheese, the more dense it is and therefore the more protein, B-group vitamins, calcium and phosphorus it will contain – and the more calories. The exception to this rule are soft cheeses, such as cream cheese and mascarpone, which are higher in calories than hard cheeses as they contain a lot of cream. These cream cheeses tend to be quite low in protein and other nutrients, because the cream itself is low in most nutrients except vitamin A.

Cheese goes well with fresh fruit,
such as apples and pears, and with
crisp celery sticks

Nutritional value of typical cheeses per 100 g (3½ oz)

	kcal	fat (g)	protein (g)	calcium (mg)
Soft fresh cheeses				
cottage cheese	98	4	13.8	73
fromage frais (8%)	113	7.1	6.8	89
mozzarella	290	22	26	590
reduced-fat soft cheese	196	15	12	360
Semi-soft rinded cheeses				
Brie	320	26	19.2	540
Goat's and sheep's milk cheeses				
feta	250	20	15.6	360
goat's cheese (medium-fat)	339	28.5	11.7	185
Semi-hard and hard cheeses				
Cheddar (traditional)	412	34	26	720
Edam	334	26	26	770
Parmesan	452	32.7	39.4	1,200
Blue cheeses				
Danish blue	348	30	20	500
Stilton	412	36	22	320

Cheese in the kitchen

Here are a few guidelines on choosing, storing and cooking.
● Buy only enough cheese to last you for about a week at a time; once cut, cheese tends to deteriorate.
● Avoid cheese that has been wrapped in cling film or similar, as it encourages a damp surface. Also, chemicals such as plasticisers in the film may transfer to the cheese.
● Keep soft fresh cheeses in the coldest part of the fridge and use within a few days of unwrapping or opening.
● Keep semi-soft, semi-hard and hard cheeses in a cool, but not too cool, place – for example, the least cold part of the fridge or a cool larder. Store either in a special cheese box with air vents, or wrapped in greaseproof paper or foil (don't wrap in cling film). Be sure not to leave any edges of cheese exposed or they will dry out and become inedible.
● If semi-soft rinded cheeses such as Brie and Camembert need to ripen a bit before being eaten, leave them (still wrapped in their original packaging) at room temperature for a few days. Once ripe, keep them in the fridge.
● Cream cheese and hard cheeses for cooking can be frozen for up to a month. Pack grated hard cheese in strong freezer bags. It is quite easy to remove just the amount you want, as the flakes stay fairly separate.
● The stronger the cheese, the less you need.
● If you want to use only a small amount of a high-fat cheese in sandwiches, make it go farther either by grating it or by cutting it thinly with a special cheese slice (available from kitchen shops). Chilling cheese before grating or slicing it will make the process easier.
● Before serving cheese as part of a cheeseboard or in a salad, bring it to room temperature, to maximise the flavour.
● Heat and prolonged cooking can spoil the texture of cheese and make it rubbery or stringy. If exposing cheese to a fierce heat, such as the grill, cook it as briefly as possible. When making a cheese sauce, add the cheese at the end of cooking and heat gently just to melt the cheese, stirring constantly.
● Add cheese to a sauce or other preparation before seasoning – most cheese is quite salty and you may find you don't need to add extra salt (taste to find out).
● If a cheese smells rancid or of ammonia, it is past its best. Cheese that tastes mouldy or rank, or that is slightly fizzy (soft cheeses), should be thrown out.

Soft cheeses and safe eating

Listeria monocytogenes is a bacterium that may be found in soft cheeses ripened using moulds, such as Brie and Camembert, and in soft blue cheeses (whether they are made from pasteurised or unpasteurised milk). The bacterium is unlikely to harm any adult in normal health, and its presence may be limited by storing and handling the cheese correctly and not keeping it beyond its sell-by date. Nevertheless, as a precaution, it is recommended that mould-ripened cheeses and soft blue cheeses are avoided by pregnant women (in whom *listeria* may cause miscarriage or premature birth), young children, the very old, the ill and people with damaged immune systems. Symptoms of listeriosis are similar to flu.

Soft fresh cheeses

These are unripened cheeses and generally need to be eaten as soon as possible after purchase. Most of them are made from cow's milk.

Cottage cheese consists of loose, soft curds mixed with a small amount of cultured cream. It has a mild, slightly sweet and tangy flavour, and is low in fat. There is also an even lower-fat version (sometimes called 'diet' cottage cheese), which has no cream added. Several flavoured varieties are also available.

Curd cheese is a low or medium-fat soft white cheese with a slightly granular texture. It is made with a lactic acid starter, which gives it a fresh, slightly sharp flavour.

Fromage frais originates from France, where it is sometimes called fromage blanc. It has a fairly dense but soft texture, making it ideal as a cream substitute. The normal (8%) version has a little cream added, whereas the 0% fat version is, as the name implies, virtually fat-free.

Mascarpone, an ultra-smooth cheese produced in Italy, has an extremely high fat content (46 g fat and 450 kcal per 100 g/ 3½ oz) because it is made from cream rather than milk.

Mozzarella, the cheese for pizza, is made differently from most soft fresh cheeses – the curds are kneaded and stretched (or spun in hot water) before being shaped into balls. This is why mozzarella has an elastic texture when melted. It is mild and delicate in flavour. Buffalo milk mozzarella and a smoked mozzarella are also available.

Paneer, a low-fat fresh cheese made in India, is usually added to curry. It is not easy to buy in the UK, but is simple to make at home (see page 110).

Quark, which originates from Germany, is a very low-fat variety of curd cheese. Its nutrient profile is similar to 0% fat fromage frais, but its flavour is slightly less creamy, and has a hint of acidity.

Ricotta, a low to medium-fat cheese, is unusual in that it is made from whey rather than curds – traditionally the whey left over after making pecorino, a hard sheep's milk cheese from Italy. Ricotta is mild and slightly sweet with a grainy, soft texture.

Soft cheese, also called cream cheese, is smooth and mild. It is available in full-fat and reduced-fat versions.

Soft and semi-soft rinded cheeses

This group includes surface-ripened cheeses, such as Brie and Camembert, which produce a downy white mould on the skin, and surface-washed cheeses, which are washed during the ripening process with various types of liquid, from salt water to brandy. They are soft or semi-soft and creamy underneath the rind, and because of their higher water content tend to be lower in fat than most hard cheeses.

Brie, from the French area of the same name, is made from full-fat or semi-skimmed cow's milk and comes in flat, round discs, which can be as large as 60 cm (2 ft) in diameter. The creamy yellow interior may be full and mild in flavour or more piquant, depending on how ripe the cheese is.

Camembert is another classic French cheese, similar to Brie but smaller and with a stronger, more tangy flavour. It is slightly lower in fat than Brie.

Neufchâtel, a full-fat cow's milk cheese from France, may be ripened only briefly to give a delicate, bloomy rind, or left to ripen until it is firm and pungent. It is available in different shapes, most famously a heart.

Port-Salut was originally made by monks in France. It is an orange rind-washed and pressed cheese with a creamy yellow interior and mild but distinctive flavour.

Taleggio could be called the Italian equivalent of Brie, with a similar nutritional profile. It has a deliciously creamy, fruity flavour with a faintly nutty aroma. Sold in oblong blocks with a pink rind, it melts well and is therefore useful in cooking.

Soft fresh cheeses (clockwise from back left): cottage cheese, fromage frais, mozzarella, curd cheese, ricotta, soft cheese, paneer, mascarpone and quark

Camembert

Brie

taleggio

Neufchâtel

Port-Salut

Cantal

Cheshire

Double Gloucester

Cheddar

Edam

Emmenthal

Gruyère

fontina

Gouda

Havarti

Semi-hard and hard cheeses

This large group contains all the cheeses that traditionally take a long time to mature. In general, the longer the maturing period, the harder and stronger the cheese will be. Some, such as Gruyère and Emmenthal, are made from scalded ('cooked') curds to produce a different texture. Most hard cheeses are pressed to help the draining process.

Cantal is a hard cheese made in the Auvergne region of France. Similar in appearance to a pale Cheddar, it may be mild, medium or strong, according to how ripe it is.

Cheddar, one of the world's greatest cheeses, originated in the Cheddar district of Somerset, but is now made all over the world. Factory-produced Cheddar tends to have an almost waxy consistency, while well-matured traditional farmhouse Cheddar has a very hard, slightly crumbly texture. The taste ranges from sweet and very mild in young cheeses to strong, sharp and savoury in those that are mature.

Cheshire is a hard English cheese that can be orange-red or white, depending on whether it has been coloured with the tasteless dye annatto. It is mild but slightly salty in flavour, with a crumbly, open texture.

Double Gloucester is a large, round English cheese made from full-fat cow's milk (Single Gloucester is made from partly skimmed milk). Like Cheshire, it is often dyed with annatto. The flavour is mild and rich, the texture smooth and creamy.

Edam, the well-known Dutch cheese, is yellowy-orange within its red or yellow wax coating. It is usually factory made, from semi-skimmed milk, and has a waxy, semi-hard texture. When young it can be quite bland, but matures to a mellow flavour.

Emmenthal, a hard, ivory-yellow Swiss or French cheese, is traditionally made from rich Alpine cow's milk. It comes in massive, brown-rinded wheels and has a waxy texture pitted with large holes. The flavour is mild, nutty and sweet.

Fontina, made from full-fat cow's milk, is a semi-hard cheese from Italy. It has a slightly nutty flavour and a creamy texture.

Gouda, produced in the Dutch town of the same name, is made from full-fat cow's milk, so it is slightly higher in fat and calories than Edam, to which it is very similar. Normally in a yellow wax coating, Gouda that has been matured for at least 7 years is coated with black wax.

Gruyère looks similar to Emmenthal but has fewer and smaller holes. Also from Switzerland, it has a stronger, nuttier flavour. Its good melting qualities make it very popular in cooking.

Havarti, from Denmark, is a semi-hard washed-rind cheese full of tiny holes. Made from full-fat cow's milk, it may be mild in flavour or strong and pungent when mature.

Lancashire is a semi-hard white cheese with a crumbly texture. Farmhouse Lancashire is made by a more laborious process than the factory version, which gives it a creamy, tangy flavour. Mass-produced Lancashire can be very bland.

Leicester is a hard cow's milk English cheese with a flaky texture. Its smooth, mellow flavour develops with age.

Parmesan, the world-famous Italian cooked, pressed cheese, is made with semi-skimmed cow's milk and is aged for at least a year (often much longer). Look for cheese marked *parmigiano reggiano* – this is the genuine article, made by traditional methods in the Emilia-Romagna region of Italy, with milk from cows fed only on grass or hay. Parmesan has a soft yellow colour, crumbly texture and slightly salty, rich taste. It is well worth buying a piece for shaving or grating, as the flavour is vastly superior to ready-grated Parmesan. It will keep for weeks in the fridge if well wrapped in foil.

Provolone is made like mozzarella. Young provolone, called *dolce*, has a very mild flavour, whereas *piccante* provolone, a hard cheese matured for up to 2 years, is much stronger and sharper. Smoked provolone is also available.

Lancashire

Leicester

Parmesan

provolone

Goat's and sheep's milk cheeses

Traditionally, goat's and sheep's milk cheeses were made in areas where the land was unsuitable for cattle, and today some of the best still come from such places – mountainous regions or countries with a dry, harsh climate. Goat's cheeses are often labelled as 'chèvre', the French word for goat. They are generally lower in fat than cow's milk cheeses and have an unmistakably 'goaty' taste. Sheep's milk cheeses are more varied, ranging in style from Roquefort to pecorino.

Fresh goat's cheese (*chèvre frais*) is unripened, has no rind and is mildly tangy in flavour.

Soft or medium-fat goat's cheese, sometimes labelled medium mature, is white-rinded with a creamy interior and a stronger

fresh goat's cheese

semi-hard goat's cheese

soft goat's cheese

feta

halloumi

pecorino

Manchego

flavour than fresh goat's cheese. It is usually log-shaped, which makes it easy to slice.

Semi-hard and hard goat's cheeses can be very pungent, with a soft and creamy or dry, crumbly interior and a firm rind. They are usually quite small – the French crottin-style cheeses can weigh as little as 25 g (scant 1 oz).

Feta, traditionally an unripened sheep's milk cheese from Greece, is now mass-produced in other countries. Much commercial feta contains a proportion of goat's and/or cow's milk and is slightly matured. White, moist and crumbly, with a piquant, salty flavour, it is sold in blocks packed in brine.

Halloumi, a medium-hard non-rinded cheese from Cyprus, has a slightly rubbery texture and a distinctive flavour that owes much to the addition of chopped mint. Like feta, halloumi is traditionally made from sheep's milk, but may now be made from a combination of milks. Unusually, it retains its shape when cooked, making it suitable for grilling or frying in slices.

Manchego, from Spain, is a hard waxed cheese sometimes pitted with tiny holes. Made from full-fat sheep's milk, it has a rich, mellow flavour with a sharp edge.

Pecorino is a hard, grainy-textured sheep's milk cheese made in Italy. The original variety is pecorino romano, which has a strong, salty flavour. Similar in character and nutritional value to Parmesan, it can be used in much the same way.

Blue cheeses

Blue cheeses are usually made by injecting the cheese with a penicillin mould in the early stages of the cheese-making process. Later, steel wires are inserted, creating tiny veins of air, which are then turned blue by the action of the mould.

Bleu d'Auvergne is a semi-hard French cheese that may be made with a mixture of cow's and goat's or sheep's milk. It has a piquant but not overly strong flavour and is usually sold wrapped in foil, since it has a very thin rind.

Cambozola, a German invention, is a creamy hybrid between Camembert and Gorgonzola. Although it is often described as blue Brie, it has a much higher fat content than Brie, since it contains added cream.

Dolcelatte, meaning 'sweet milk' in Italian, is the brand name of a creamy, mild commercial version of Gorgonzola.

Stilton

Shropshire blue

Roquefort

Dolcelatte

bleu d'Auvergne

Cambozola

Gorgonzola

Gorgonzola is a semi-hard cow's milk cheese from central Italy, with a slightly crumbly texture. Mass-produced versions can be quite mild, while farmhouse ones are more pungent.

Shropshire blue is deep orange-yellow with blue veining. Its strong, salty taste has an underlying hint of sweetness.

Roquefort comes from the region of the same name in France, where it is matured in limestone caves. A full-flavoured yet subtle, semi-soft blue cheese, with a smooth, creamy texture, it is made from full-fat sheep's milk. It is almost rindless.

Stilton, often described as the king of English cheeses, is a semi-hard, unpressed cheese made from full-fat cow's milk, traditionally with cream added. It varies in strength depending on how long it has been matured, but the flavour should be rich and piquant rather than sharp. Traditional farmhouse Stilton, moulded into tall cylinders, is strongest of all, with more grey-green veining than younger cheeses. Stilton can only be made in certain areas of central England.

To Start the Day

Great dishes for breakfast or brunch

It is difficult to imagine the first meal of the day without eggs or milk in some form. These staple foods are an extremely nutritious way to break the night's fast, either on their own – simply as boiled or scrambled eggs with toast, for example, or as milk with cereal – or turned into more substantial dishes. Eggs and milk make the batter for American-style pancakes and waffles, delicious with bacon and mushrooms or with fresh fruit. Poached eggs can be served atop tortillas with a salsa or on English muffins with a yogurt hollandaise.

Milk can moisten oats for muesli, or be whizzed with yogurt, banana and orange juice into a high-energy meal-in-a-glass milk shake.

Scrambled eggs with smoked salmon and dill

Here's a great new way to scramble eggs – cooked in a double saucepan or in a bowl over simmering water, without any butter, then mixed with crème fraîche for a deliciously creamy result. With strips of smoked salmon and fresh dill added, and served on wholemeal toast, this is the ultimate luxury brunch dish.

Serves 4

6 eggs

3 tbsp semi-skimmed milk

6 plum tomatoes, halved lengthways

4 thick slices wholemeal bread

3 tbsp crème fraîche

75 g (2½ oz) sliced smoked salmon, cut into thin strips

1 tsp lemon juice

1 tbsp chopped fresh dill

salt and pepper

sprigs of fresh dill to garnish

Preparation time: 10 minutes

Cooking time: 10 minutes

Each serving provides

kcal 363, protein 22 g, fat 21 g (of which saturated fat 9 g), carbohydrate 24 g (of which sugars 6 g), fibre 4 g

✓✓✓	A, B$_{12}$
✓✓	C, E, niacin, selenium, zinc
✓	B$_1$, B$_2$, B$_6$, folate, calcium, copper, iron, potassium

1 Lightly beat the eggs with the milk in a heatproof bowl or in the top of a double saucepan. Set over a saucepan containing barely simmering water – the base of the bowl or pan should just touch the water. Cook for 6–8 minutes or until the eggs begin to thicken, stirring frequently.

2 Preheat the grill to high. While the eggs are cooking, arrange the tomatoes cut side up on the rack of the grill pan, and sprinkle them with a little salt and pepper. Add the slices of bread to the rack. Grill for 4–5 minutes, turning the bread over halfway through, until the tomatoes are lightly browned and the bread is toasted on both sides.

3 Add the crème fraîche to the eggs, and season to taste with salt and pepper. Cook for a further 1 minute, stirring constantly, until the mixture is softly scrambled. Sprinkle the smoked salmon with the lemon juice, then add to the eggs together with the chopped dill. Immediately remove from the heat.

4 Place the toast on warmed serving plates and divide the smoked salmon scramble among them. Garnish each with a sprig of dill. Add 3 grilled tomato halves to each plate, and serve.

Some more ideas

● Serve on slices of pumpernickel bread.

● For a ham and egg scramble, replace the salmon with smoked ham, and use chopped fresh flat-leaf parsley instead of dill.

● Make Parsee scrambled eggs, a spicy Indian version. Melt 15 g (½ oz) butter in a non-stick saucepan, and gently sauté 2 tsp grated fresh root ginger, 1 seeded and finely chopped fresh red chilli, and ¼ tsp each ground cumin and ground coriander for 1 minute. Stir in the egg and milk mixture, and cook over a low heat, stirring constantly, until softly scrambled. Stir in 3 tbsp Greek-style yogurt, 4 chopped tomatoes and 1 tbsp chopped fresh coriander. Serve hot, with warm naan bread.

Plus points

● Eggs are a highly nutritious food, and provide many essential nutrients in a very convenient package. In addition to high-quality protein, eggs contain useful amounts of vitamins A, B$_2$, B$_{12}$, E and niacin, and plenty of minerals.

● Salmon contains omega-3 fatty acids, a type of polyunsaturated fat that can help to protect against heart disease and strokes.

Huevos rancheros

For a fun weekend brunch, serve this Mexican-style dish of poached eggs, warm flour tortillas, a fresh tomato and chilli salsa, and toppings of grated cheese, soured cream, spring onions and fresh coriander.

Serves 4

4 large or 8 small flour tortillas, about 160 g
   (5¾ oz) in total

1 tsp vinegar

4 eggs

85 g (3 oz) Edam cheese, coarsely grated

6 tbsp soured cream

4 spring onions, chopped

chopped fresh coriander to garnish

lime wedges to serve

Tomato and chilli salsa

5 tomatoes, finely chopped

1 plump, mild fresh red chilli, seeded and
   finely chopped

½ small red onion, finely chopped

1 small garlic clove, finely chopped

2 tbsp finely chopped fresh coriander

1 tbsp extra virgin olive oil

2–3 tsp lime juice, to taste

salt and pepper

Preparation and cooking time: 35 minutes, plus
   30 minutes marinating

Each serving provides Ⓥ

kcal 471, **protein** 21 g, **fat** 20 g (of which
saturated fat 8 g), **carbohydrate** 55 g (of
which sugars 6 g), **fibre** 3 g

✓✓✓	A, B$_{12}$
✓✓	C, E, niacin, calcium, zinc
✓	B$_1$, B$_2$, B$_6$, folate, copper, iron, potassium, selenium

1 First make the salsa. Place the chopped tomatoes in a bowl and stir in the chilli, red onion, garlic and coriander. Add the oil and lime juice to taste. Set aside to marinate for about 30 minutes, then season with salt and pepper to taste.

2 Preheat the oven to 180°C (350°F, gas mark 4). Wrap the stacked-up tortillas in foil and put them in the oven to warm for 10 minutes, or according to the packet instructions.

3 Meanwhile, half fill a frying pan with water. Heat until just starting to simmer, then reduce the heat so the water does not boil. Add the vinegar. Break the eggs into the water, one at a time, and poach for 3–4 minutes. Towards the end of cooking, spoon the water over the yolks. When cooked, remove the eggs with a draining spoon and drain on kitchen paper.

4 Place the warmed tortillas on plates (1 large or 2 small ones each). Spoon over a little salsa, then put the eggs on top and season with salt and pepper to taste. Let everyone help themselves to the rest of the salsa, the grated cheese, soured cream and spring onions, plus chopped coriander for sprinkling over the top and lime wedges for squeezing.

Another idea

● Add quick home-made refried beans, for a very hearty brunch dish. Heat 1 tbsp sunflower oil in a saucepan. Add 1 finely chopped garlic clove and ¼ tsp ground cumin, and cook for a few seconds. Stir in 1 can of pinto or borlotti beans, about 410 g, drained, and 120 ml (4 fl oz) water. Cover and simmer for 5 minutes or until the beans are soft enough to mash. Roughly mash them with a fork, then cook uncovered for a further 3 minutes. If the mixture is too liquid, cook for a few more minutes. Season with salt to taste.

Plus points

● Tortillas, or wraps, are a great alternative to commonly eaten breads, and are another way to boost starchy carbohydrate intake.

● Tomatoes are a rich source of vitamin C, most of which is concentrated in the jellylike substance around the seeds.

Herbed French toast

Give breakfast or brunch a new twist with this savoury version of French toast, also called pain perdu or eggy bread. Triangles of bread are dipped into a fresh herb and egg mixture, then pan-fried until crisp and golden. Serve with big and 'meaty' portobella mushrooms and lean bacon, both grilled, for a really tasty combination.

Serves 4

4 large eggs
4 tbsp semi-skimmed milk
1 tbsp finely chopped parsley
1 tbsp finely chopped fresh chives
½ tbsp chopped fresh thyme, or a pinch of dried thyme
pinch of paprika (optional)
4 large portobella mushrooms or large flat mushrooms, about 250 g (8½ oz) in total
3 tbsp sunflower oil
4 rashers lean back bacon, rinded and trimmed of fat
5 thick slices white bread
salt and pepper

Preparation and cooking time: about 25 minutes

Each serving provides

kcal 349, protein 19 g, fat 19 g (of which saturated fat 4 g), carbohydrate 28 g (of which sugars 2 g), fibre 2 g

✓✓✓	B$_{12}$, copper, selenium
✓✓	B$_1$, B$_2$, E, niacin, zinc
✓	A, B$_6$, folate, calcium, iron, potassium

1 Combine the eggs, milk, most of the parsley, the chives, thyme and paprika, if using, in a shallow dish. Season to taste. Set aside.

2 Preheat the grill to moderately high. Remove the stalks from the mushrooms. Using 1 tbsp of the oil, lightly brush the gill sides of the mushroom caps. Place them gill side up on the grill rack. Add the bacon rashers to the grill rack. Grill the mushrooms for 6–7 minutes and the bacon for about 10 minutes, turning the rashers over halfway through. When the mushrooms and bacon are cooked, remove from the grill pan and keep warm.

3 Meanwhile, cut each slice of bread into 4 triangles. Heat a large, non-stick frying pan over a moderate heat and add 1 tbsp of the remaining oil. Dip about one-third of the bread triangles into the egg mixture to moisten on both sides, then put into the hot pan. Cook for 1–2 minutes or until golden brown on both sides. Remove from the pan and keep warm while you cook the rest of the bread in the same way, adding the remaining 1 tbsp oil as needed.

4 To serve, arrange 5 triangles of French toast on each plate. Cut the mushrooms into thick slices and add to the plates, together with the bacon. Sprinkle with the remaining parsley.

Another idea

● For sweet orange French toast, first make a fresh fruit compote to serve alongside, in place of the bacon and mushrooms. Combine 250 g (8½ oz) raspberries and 2 thinly sliced ripe peaches in a bowl. Cover and set aside. Gently whisk 3 large eggs with 3 tbsp semi-skimmed milk and the finely grated zest of 1 large orange. Cut 8 slices of brioche loaf, each about 5 mm (¼ in) thick, then cut each slice in half. Dip into the egg mixture and cook in batches as in the main recipe. Serve the hot French toast topped with the fruit compote and 1 tbsp Greek-style yogurt per serving.

Plus points

● This hearty breakfast dish contains fewer calories than the traditional version, which is often served with melting butter and maple or golden syrup.

● Wholemeal bread is considered to be healthier than white bread, but in fact all breads are important sources of starchy carbohydrate. Also, white bread has calcium added and subsequently contains more of this important mineral than wholemeal bread.

American buttermilk pancakes

American pancakes are thick, like a drop scone, and wonderfully light and fluffy. They can be left plain, but adding fruit, such as sliced banana, makes them infinitely more exciting, and more nutritious too. Here they are served with cinnamon-spiced yogurt and a drizzle of honey. Serve straight from the pan, to enjoy at their best.

Serves 6 (makes 12 pancakes)

115 g (4 oz) self-raising white flour
115 g (4 oz) self-raising wholemeal flour
pinch of salt
30 g (1 oz) caster sugar
2 large eggs, separated
300 ml (10 fl oz) buttermilk
1 large banana, thinly sliced
1½ tsp sunflower oil

To serve
6 tbsp Greek-style yogurt
¼ tsp ground cinnamon
6 tsp clear honey

Preparation time: 20 minutes
Cooking time: 15–20 minutes

Each serving provides

kcal 340, **protein** 11 g, **fat** 10 g (of which saturated fat 3 g), **carbohydrate** 57 g (of which sugars 30 g), **fibre** 2.5 g

✓✓	calcium
✓	A, B₁, B₂, B₆, B₁₂, E, copper, iron, potassium, selenium, zinc

1 Sift the white and wholemeal flours and the salt into a large bowl, and tip in the bran left in the sieve. Stir in the sugar. Mix the egg yolks with the buttermilk and 1 tbsp cold water. Gradually beat into the flour mixture to make a very thick batter.

2 Whisk the egg whites in a separate bowl until light and fluffy. Fold into the batter, then fold in the banana.

3 Heat a griddle or a large, heavy-based, non-stick frying pan over a moderate heat, then lightly grease with a little of the oil. Spoon large, heaped spoonfuls of the batter onto the hot griddle or pan, spacing them well apart. You'll probably be able to cook 3 or 4 at a time, depending on the size of the griddle or pan.

4 Cook for 1–2 minutes or until golden and firm on the underside and bubbles appear on the surface. Flip the pancakes over using a large palette knife, and cook on the other side for 1–2 minutes. Remove from the pan and keep warm while cooking the rest of the pancakes, lightly greasing the griddle or pan with more oil between each batch.

5 Mix the yogurt with the cinnamon. Place 2 warm pancakes on each serving plate, add 1 tbsp of spiced yogurt and drizzle over 1 tsp honey. Serve immediately.

Some more ideas

• If buttermilk is unavailable, you can use 300 ml (10 fl oz) semi-skimmed milk mixed with 1 tsp lemon juice.
• Use all white flour and no wholemeal.
• Add 2–3 tbsp sultanas or raisins with the bananas.
• For blueberry pancakes, make the batter with 225 g (8 oz) self-raising white flour and sift it with 1 tsp ground allspice. Add 170 g (6 oz) fresh blueberries to the batter instead of the banana. Serve with a mixed berry salad (see Blueberry popovers on page 44).
• Make blackberry pancakes by adding 170 g (6 oz) fresh blackberries instead of the banana.

Plus points

• Buttermilk is traditionally the liquid left over after the creamy part of milk has been turned into butter by churning. Nowadays, though, buttermilk is usually made by adding a culture to skimmed milk. Whichever way it is made, buttermilk is very low in fat.
• Bananas provide readily absorbed carbohydrate as well as potassium, a mineral essential for the proper functioning of nerves, muscles and, indeed, all cells in the body. They are a fruit particularly popular with children, so this recipe makes a great healthy breakfast for young appetites.

Pecan waffles with maple, pear and blackberry sauce

Crisp, crunchy waffles, so popular in France, Belgium and North America, are a lovely treat for breakfast or brunch. To make these, you will need a waffle iron that can be used on the hob or an electric waffle maker.

Serves 4 (makes 4–8 waffles, depending on the size of the waffle iron)

125 g (4½ oz) plain flour
½ tsp ground cinnamon
1 tsp baking powder
1 tbsp caster sugar
1 large egg, separated
200 ml (7 fl oz) semi-skimmed milk
15 g (½ oz) butter, melted
15 g (½ oz) pecan nuts, finely chopped

Maple, pear and blackberry sauce

1 large, ripe dessert pear
4 tbsp maple syrup
50 g (1¾ oz) pecan nut halves
100 g (3½ oz) blackberries

Preparation time: 20 minutes
Cooking time: 10–15 minutes

Each serving provides Ⓥ

kcal 413, **protein** 9 g, **fat** 18 g (of which saturated fat 4 g), **carbohydrate** 58 g (of which sugars 32 g), **fibre** 3 g

✓✓	copper, zinc
✓	A, B₁, B₂, B₁₂, E, niacin, calcium, iron, potassium

1 First make the maple and fruit sauce. Cut the pear lengthways into quarters and cut out the core, then cut the pear into fine dice. Put into a small heavy saucepan and add the maple syrup. Warm gently, then remove the pan from the heat. Stir in the pecan nut halves and the blackberries. Set aside while making the waffles.

2 Heat and lightly grease the waffle iron or maker according to the manufacturer's instructions.

3 Meanwhile, make the waffle batter. Sift the flour, cinnamon, baking powder and sugar into a medium-sized mixing bowl. Make a well in the centre, and add the egg yolk and milk to the well. Gently whisk the egg yolk and milk together, then gradually whisk in the flour to make a thick, smooth batter. Whisk in the melted butter, then stir in the finely chopped pecans.

4 Whisk the egg white in a separate bowl until stiff. Pile it on top of the batter and, using a large metal spoon, fold it in gently.

5 Spoon a small ladleful (3–4 tbsp) of batter into the centre of the hot waffle iron or maker, then close the lid tightly. If using a waffle iron on top of the hob, cook for about 30 seconds,

then turn the waffle iron over and cook for another 30 seconds. Open the waffle iron: the waffle should be golden brown on both sides and should come away easily from the iron. (If using an electric waffle maker, follow the manufacturer's instructions – usually allow 2–3 minutes for each waffle.)

6 Lift the cooked waffle from the iron using a round-bladed knife, and keep warm while cooking the rest of the waffles.

7 Just before all the waffles are ready, gently warm the fruit sauce, then pour into a sauceboat or serving bowl. Serve with the warm waffles.

Plus points

● Pears are a good source of soluble fibre in the form of pectin. Soluble fibre can help to lower blood cholesterol levels.

● Maple syrup, extracted from the sap of the maple tree, is a delicious sweetener. It contains useful amounts of zinc.

Some more ideas

● To keep the waffles warm, spread them in a single layer on a rack in a very low oven.

● Use walnuts instead of pecans, and either maple syrup or clear honey in the sauce.

● For savoury Parmesan waffles, to serve as a hearty brunch dish, omit the cinnamon, sugar and pecans from the batter. Instead, sift the flour with a good pinch each of black pepper and cayenne pepper, and salt to taste. Add

2 tbsp freshly grated Parmesan cheese before folding in the egg white. Instead of serving with the maple and fruit sauce, top each serving of waffles with a poached egg (see page 14) and scatter over some snipped fresh chives.

High-vitality milk shake

This satisfying 'breakfast in a glass' is made with milk and thick yogurt flavoured with banana and freshly squeezed orange juice, plus some wheatgerm for extra vitamin value. A milk shake-style drink makes a great energising start to the day, ideal for people in a hurry or those who aren't keen to eat much in the morning.

Serves 2

300 ml (10 fl oz) semi-skimmed milk, chilled
200 g (7 oz) Greek-style yogurt
juice of 1 large orange
1 large banana, sliced
1 tsp clear honey
1 tbsp wheatgerm

Preparation time: 5 minutes

1 Place all the ingredients in a blender or food processor and whizz for a couple of minutes until smooth and creamy.

2 Pour into 2 tall glasses and enjoy immediately, while the milk shake is still frothy.

Some more ideas

● Make a berry milk shake using 170 g (6 oz) strawberries instead of banana (this is shown on the left in the picture). Raspberries are good too, or try the chopped flesh of 1 mango.

● Replace the wheatgerm with 1 tbsp ground sunflower seeds (grind them in a coffee grinder or with a pestle and mortar).

● Use vanilla frozen yogurt instead of Greek-style yogurt.

● Make a mixed fruit shake with frozen yogurt. Combine 300 ml (10 fl oz) semi-skimmed milk, 200 g (7 oz) strawberry frozen yogurt, 1 large sliced banana, 1 skinned and chopped peach and 2 tbsp rolled oats in a blender or food processor, and whizz until creamy and frothy. Serve immediately.

Plus points

● Milk is an important source of vitamin B_2. This vitamin is sensitive to ultraviolet light, so milk should be brought in from the doorstep as soon as possible after delivery.

● Greek-style yogurt may seem rich and creamy in taste, but a level tbsp contains only 17 kcal. By comparison, a level tbsp of double cream contains 67 kcal.

● The addition of wheatgerm boosts the content of vitamin E and B vitamins in this recipe, and orange juice provides vitamin C, so this is truly a 'high-vitality' drink.

Each serving provides Ⓥ

kcal 307, **protein** 14 g, **fat** 12 g (of which saturated fat 7 g), **carbohydrate** 38 g (of which sugars 36 g), **fibre** 1 g

✓✓✓	calcium
✓✓	B_2, B_{12}, C, zinc
✓	A, B_1, B_6, E, folate, niacin, potassium

Blueberry popovers

Similar to Yorkshire puddings, popovers are a much-loved American classic, and the sweet version here is perfect for breakfast or brunch. The batter is baked, with fresh blueberries added, in deep muffin or Yorkshire pudding tins, and the popovers are served with sweet, fresh berries to add extra vitamin C.

Serves 4 (makes 8 popovers)
1 tsp butter
125 g (4½ oz) plain flour
pinch of salt
1 tsp caster sugar
2 eggs
250 ml (8½ fl oz) semi-skimmed milk
75 g (2½ oz) blueberries
1 tbsp icing sugar to dust
Mixed berry salad
150 g (5½ oz) raspberries
100 g (3½ oz) blueberries
200 g (7 oz) strawberries, thickly sliced
1 tbsp icing sugar, or to taste

Preparation time: 20 minutes
Cooking time: 25–30 minutes

1 Preheat the oven to 220°C (425°F, gas mark 7). Using a piece of crumpled kitchen paper and the butter, lightly grease 8 of the cups in a deep, non-stick muffin tray. Each cup should measure 6 cm (2½ in) across the top and be 2.5 cm (1 in) deep.

2 To make the popovers, sift the flour, salt and caster sugar into a mixing bowl and make a well in the centre. Break the eggs into the well, add the milk and beat together with a fork.

3 Using a wire whisk, gradually work the flour into the liquid to make a smooth batter that has the consistency of single cream. Pour into a large jug.

4 Divide the batter evenly among the prepared muffin cups – they should be about two-thirds full. With a spoon, drop a few blueberries into the batter in each cup, dividing them equally.

5 Bake in the middle of the oven for 25–30 minutes or until the popovers are golden brown, well risen and crisp around the edges.

6 Meanwhile, make the berry salad. Purée 100 g (3½ oz) of the raspberries by pressing them through a nylon sieve into a bowl. Add the rest of the raspberries to the bowl, together with the blueberries and strawberries. Sift the icing sugar over the fruit and fold gently to mix everything together.

7 Unmould the popovers with the help of a round-bladed knife, and dust with the icing sugar. Serve hot, with the berry salad.

Some more ideas
• Use frozen blueberries, thawed and well drained. You can use thawed frozen raspberries and blueberries for the berry salad, too.
• For a baked sweet batter pudding, make the batter as in the main recipe, then add 4 tbsp fizzy mineral water or cold water. Pour into a 1.4–1.7 litre (2½–3 pint) shallow baking dish that has been lightly greased with butter (omit the blueberries). Bake for 30–35 minutes or until crisp and well risen. Spoon the berry salad into the centre of the hot pudding, scatter over 2 tbsp toasted flaked almonds, dust with the icing sugar and serve immediately.

Plus points
• Blueberries, like cranberries, contain antibacterial compounds called anthocyanins. These are effective against the *E. coli* bacteria that cause gastrointestinal disorders and urinary tract infections.
• Weight for weight, strawberries contain more vitamin C than oranges, and more than other berries such as raspberries.

Each serving provides Ⓥ
kcal 243, **protein** 10 g, **fat** 6 g (of which saturated fat 2 g), **carbohydrate** 40 g (of which sugars 16 g), **fibre** 3 g

✓✓✓	C
✓✓	B₁₂
✓	A, B₁, B₂, folate, niacin, calcium, copper, iron, potassium, zinc

Eggs Benedict

Created in the 1920s at Delmonico's restaurant in New York City, this dish traditionally uses ham or bacon and a rich butter sauce. Here, a lower-fat yogurt and chive hollandaise contrasts with the richness of poached eggs and lean Parma ham, to make a lighter, but equally special version.

Serves 4

1 tsp vinegar

4 eggs

4 English muffins, halved

4 slices Parma ham, about 55 g (2 oz) in total, trimmed of fat

salt and pepper

Yogurt and chive hollandaise sauce

2 egg yolks

1 tsp Dijon mustard

150 g (5½ oz) Greek-style yogurt

1 tbsp snipped fresh chives

To garnish

paprika

1 tbsp snipped fresh chives

Preparation and cooking time: 25 minutes

1 First make the hollandaise sauce. Whisk together the egg yolks, mustard and yogurt in a heatproof bowl or in the top of a double saucepan. Set over a saucepan of barely simmering water and cook for 12–15 minutes, stirring constantly, until thick – the sauce will become thinner at first, but will then thicken. Stir in the chives, and season with salt and pepper to taste. Remove from the heat and keep the sauce warm over the pan of hot water.

2 Half fill a frying pan with water. Bring to the boil, then add the vinegar. Reduce the heat so the water is just simmering gently, then carefully break the eggs into the water, one at a time. Poach for 3–4 minutes, spooning the hot water over the yolks towards the end of cooking.

3 Meanwhile, preheat the grill to high. Lightly toast the muffin halves for about 1 minute on each side. Place one half on each of 4 warmed plates and top each with a slice of Parma ham, crumpled slightly to fit.

4 Using a draining spoon, remove the poached eggs from the pan, one at a time. Rest on kitchen paper to drain off any water and, if liked, trim off any ragged edges of egg white with scissors. Place an egg on top of each ham-topped muffin half.

5 Spoon the warm hollandaise sauce over the eggs, and sprinkle each serving with a pinch of paprika and chives. Serve immediately, with the remaining toasted muffin halves.

Each serving provides

kcal 453, **protein** 22 g, **fat** 22 g (of which saturated fat 5 g), **carbohydrate** 46 g (of which sugars 21 g), **fibre** 7 g

✓✓✓	B$_{12}$, zinc
✓✓	A, B$_2$, niacin, calcium, copper, iron
✓	B$_6$, E, folate, potassium, selenium

Plus points

● All the fat in eggs is found in the yolk – approximately 6 g per egg – and it is predominantly unsaturated fat.

● Parma ham is the most famous of the Italian prosciuttos. It is a good lean alternative to bacon, especially if, as in this recipe, all visible fat is trimmed away.

● Chives belong to the same family as onions and garlic. They are believed to stimulate the appetite and act as a tonic, probably because of their sulphur content.

Some more ideas

- Use thin slices of lean cooked ham instead of Parma ham.
- Instead of chives, add 1 tbsp chopped fresh tarragon or 30 g (1 oz) chopped watercress to the hollandaise, and garnish with sprigs of tarragon or watercress.
- For egg crostini, toast 8 thin slices of ciabatta bread under a preheated moderate grill until lightly golden on both sides. Rub a cut garlic clove lightly over the surface, then discard the garlic. Thinly slice 3 plum tomatoes and arrange on top of the toasts. Put 2 toasts on each plate. Make the hollandaise sauce as in the main recipe, but adding a small pinch of saffron threads or powder at the start of cooking and omitting the chives; keep the sauce warm. Heat 15 g (½ oz) butter in a non-stick frying pan and sauté 225 g (8 oz) mixed wild mushrooms, sliced if large, for 3–4 minutes or until tender. Stir in 1 tbsp snipped fresh chives. Spoon over the top of the tomatoes and top each serving with a poached egg. Drizzle over the hollandaise sauce and serve immediately.

Fruity Bircher muesli

The original recipe for this nutritious breakfast cereal was developed over a century ago, by Dr Bircher-Benner at his clinic in Zurich. The technique of soaking the cereal, here using milk, makes it easier to digest, and also easier to eat. Try it not just for breakfast, but as a sustaining snack at any time of day.

Serves 4

115 g (4 oz) rolled oats

115 g (4 oz) sultanas

250 ml (8½ fl oz) semi-skimmed milk

1 crisp dessert apple, such as Cox's

2 tsp lemon juice

30 g (1 oz) hazelnuts, roughly chopped

15 g (½ oz) pumpkin seeds

1 tbsp sesame seeds

100 g (3½ oz) strawberries, chopped

4 tbsp plain low-fat bio yogurt

4 tsp clear honey

Preparation time: 10 minutes, plus overnight soaking

1 Place the oats and sultanas in a large bowl and add the milk. Stir to mix evenly, then cover and place in the refrigerator. Leave to soak overnight.

2 The next day, just before eating, grate the apple, discarding the core. Toss the apple with the lemon juice to prevent browning.

3 Stir the hazelnuts, pumpkin seeds and sesame seeds into the oat mixture, then stir in the grated apple and strawberries.

4 To serve, divide the muesli among 4 cereal bowls, and top each with a spoonful of yogurt and honey.

Another idea

- To make a mixed grain muesli, soak 25 g (scant 1 oz) rolled oats, 45 g (1½ oz) malted wheat flakes, 30 g (1 oz) flaked rice and 115 g (4 oz) raisins in 250 ml (8½ fl oz) buttermilk. Just before eating, stir in 25 g (scant 1 oz) roughly chopped almonds and 20 g (¾ oz) sunflower seeds, then add 1 roughly mashed banana and 1 chopped mango. Serve topped with plain low-fat bio yogurt.

Plus points

- Yogurt is usually made by introducing 2 harmless bacteria into milk. Bio yogurts, which are made by using a slightly different bacterium, are believed to be more effective at keeping a healthier balance of bacteria in the gut than other yogurts.
- Oats have a low glycaemic index, which means they are digested and absorbed slowly and so produce a gentle, sustained rise in blood glucose levels.
- Hazelnuts are a particularly good source of vitamin E and most of the B vitamins, apart from B_{12}. Like most other nuts, they have a high fat content; however, this is mostly the more beneficial monounsaturated fat.

Each serving provides ⓥ

kcal 366, **protein** 11 g, **fat** 12 g (of which saturated fat 2 g), **carbohydrate** 56 g (of which sugars 37 g), **fibre** 4 g

✓✓	B_1, C, E, calcium, copper, zinc
✓	B_2, B_6, B_{12}, folate, niacin, iron, potassium

Sweet couscous

Couscous is extremely versatile and can be used for both savoury dishes and for sweet ones, such as this quickly made, delicious hot cereal. The couscous is mixed with dried fruit and soaked briefly in hot milk, then topped with fresh fruit, to create something a little different to start the day – a great alternative to porridge.

Serves 4

225 g (8 oz) couscous

85 g (3 oz) raisins

85 g (3 oz) ready-to-eat stoned prunes, chopped

finely grated zest of 1 small orange

750 ml (1¼ pints) semi-skimmed milk

To serve

2 nectarines, sliced

8 tbsp fromage frais

Preparation and cooking time: about 20 minutes

1 Put the couscous in a bowl with the raisins, prunes and orange zest, and stir to mix thoroughly.

2 Pour the milk into a saucepan and bring just to the boil. Pour the hot milk over the couscous mixture, stirring well, then cover with foil or a folded clean tea-towel. Leave to soak for about 10 minutes or until the couscous is plumped up and all the milk has been absorbed.

3 Spoon the couscous into bowls and top with sliced nectarines and fromage frais. Serve immediately.

Some more ideas

• Instead of raisins and prunes, use other dried fruit such as ready-to-eat dried pears or peaches.

• Use the finely grated zest of 1 small pink grapefruit or 1 lemon rather than orange zest.

• Serve with extra semi-skimmed milk or low-fat plain yogurt rather than fromage frais.

• Make sweet polenta, another delicious alternative to porridge. Heat 1 litre (1¾ pints) semi-skimmed milk in a saucepan until boiling. Gradually stir in 170 g (6 oz) instant polenta, then cook gently, stirring constantly, for about 5 minutes or until the mixture thickens and all the milk has been absorbed. Fold in 85 g (3 oz) dried cranberries and 85 g (3 oz) chopped ready-to-eat dried apricots or figs. Sweeten the mixture with 2 tbsp clear honey and flavour with 1 tsp ground mixed spice or cinnamon. Serve hot, with sliced fresh oranges or with extra milk.

Plus points

• Fromage frais, a soft cheese originally from France, makes an excellent low-fat alternative to cream for topping this cereal.

• Prunes have a lot to offer nutritionally, being a good source of fibre as well as providing several vitamins, minerals and phytochemicals. They are known to have a laxative effect, so can be helpful in treating constipation.

Each serving provides Ⓥ

kcal 397, **protein** 15 g, **fat** 8 g (of which saturated fat 4 g), **carbohydrate** 70 g (of which sugars 41 g), **fibre** 2.5 g

✓✓✓ B_{12}

✓✓ B_2, C, calcium, iron

✓ A, B_1, B_6, niacin, copper, potassium, selenium, zinc

For Maximum Vitality

Fresh combinations with fruit and vegetables

Salads, snacks and dips based on eggs, cheese and yogurt become even more nutritious when partnered with plenty of fresh fruit and vegetables. Gruyère cheese is perfectly complemented by spinach, mushrooms, cherry tomatoes and strips of smoked ham, while Roquefort is divine with pears, watercress and walnuts. Or try a pretty salad of stuffed eggs on a bed of carrot and courgette ribbons. Slices of toasted ciabatta topped with mozzarella, peppers and fennel makes a great lunch, as does a garlicky yogurt and roasted aubergine dip served with crudités.

Turkish aubergine and yogurt dip

Many versions of this creamy aubergine dip are to be found around the Mediterranean. This one is thickened with ground almonds, which add both texture and protein. Served with pitta bread and crunchy vegetable crudités, the dip makes a delicious snack or starter for 8, or a well-balanced lunch dish for 4.

Serves 8

3 aubergines, about 675 g (1½ lb) in total

2 large garlic cloves

30 g (1 oz) ground almonds

1 tbsp lemon juice

1 tsp ground cumin

1 tbsp extra virgin olive oil

150 g (5½ oz) Greek-style yogurt

50 g (1¾ oz) stoned black olives, roughly chopped

salt and pepper

To serve

3 courgettes

3 celery sticks

½ cauliflower, broken into large florets

8 wholemeal pitta breads

To garnish

¼ tsp paprika

4 black olives, halved and stoned

Preparation and cooking time: about 1½ hours, plus 15 minutes draining

Each serving provides

kcal 188, **protein** 8 g, **fat** 7 g (of which saturated fat 2 g), **carbohydrate** 25 g (of which sugars 5 g), **fibre** 5 g

✓✓	C
✓	A, B₁, B₆, E, folate, niacin, calcium, copper, iron, potassium, zinc

1 Preheat the oven to 180°C (350°F, gas mark 4). Prick the aubergines in several places with a fork and place on a lightly greased baking tray. Roast for 40 minutes, turning the aubergines occasionally. Add the unpeeled garlic cloves to the baking tray and continue roasting for 20 minutes or until the aubergines feel very soft.

2 Remove from the oven and leave the aubergines until they are cool enough to handle, then cut them into quarters lengthways. Strip off the skin and put the flesh into a colander. Leave to drain for about 15 minutes.

3 Squeeze out as much liquid from the aubergine flesh as possible. Squeeze the roasted garlic cloves from their skin. Combine the aubergine flesh, garlic, almonds, lemon juice, cumin and olive oil in a food processor, and purée until smooth. Alternatively, put the ingredients in a bowl and purée using a hand-held blender.

4 Stir in the yogurt and chopped olives. Season with salt and pepper to taste. Cover and set aside.

5 Preheat a ridged cast-iron grill pan, or preheat the grill to high. Cut the courgettes and celery into finger-length sticks suitable for dipping and arrange on a platter with the cauliflower florets. Put the pitta breads on the grill pan or under the grill and toast for 2–3 minutes on each side or until just beginning to brown. Cut each bread into 6 wedges and place on the platter.

6 Sprinkle the aubergine dip with paprika and garnish with the halved olives. Serve with the vegetable crudités and warm pitta breads.

Plus points

• In most recipes, aubergines are fried and they are notorious for soaking up the frying fat. For this dish they are dry-roasted, which keeps the overall fat content low.

• Garlic is not just a valuable ingredient in the kitchen, its medicinal properties have been recognised for centuries. Naturopaths and herbalists use it to treat dozens of ailments, from athlete's foot to colds.

• Olives are low in calories – just 30 kcal in 30 g (1 oz), which is about 10 olives – and most of the fat they contain is the healthy monounsaturated type. They are also a source of vitamin E.

for maximum vitality

Some more ideas

- The aubergine dip can be made 1–2 hours in advance and kept in the fridge. Let it return to room temperature before serving.
- For a Moroccan white bean and yogurt dip, drain and rinse 2 cans of cannellini beans, about 410 g each. Put them in a food processor with 2 tbsp tahini, 1 tbsp lemon juice, ¼ tsp ground cumin and ¼ tsp ground coriander, and process until smooth. Alternatively, combine the ingredients in a bowl and purée using a hand-held blender. Stir in 150 g (5½ oz) Greek-style yogurt, 2 tbsp chopped fresh coriander, 1 tbsp chopped fresh mint, and salt and pepper to taste. Garnish with a sprig of fresh mint, and serve with sesame breadsticks or Arab flat bread, and crudités of cucumber and carrot sticks, and red and yellow pepper strips.

Gruyère, ham and mushroom salad

The Swiss cheese Gruyère is usually used for cooking, but its sweet, nutty taste makes it the perfect choice for a salad, too. It works well with lean ham, green beans, cherry tomatoes and salad leaves in a piquant lemon and green peppercorn dressing, to make this super lunch dish. Serve with warm crusty bread.

Serves 4

200 g (7 oz) fine green beans

115 g (4 oz) Gruyère cheese, any rind removed

85 g (3 oz) thickly sliced lean smoked ham, trimmed of fat

125 g (4½ oz) cherry tomatoes, halved

225 g (8 oz) baby button mushrooms, sliced

85 g (3 oz) watercress

45 g (1½ oz) baby spinach leaves

45 g (1½ oz) rocket

2 tbsp snipped fresh chives

Green peppercorn dressing

3 tbsp sunflower oil

grated zest and juice of 1 lemon

1 tbsp dried green peppercorns, crushed

2 tsp clear honey

salt

Preparation and cooking time: 25 minutes

1 Cook the beans in a saucepan of boiling water for 4 minutes or until just tender. Drain and refresh under cold running water.

2 To make the dressing, place the oil, lemon zest and juice, peppercorns, honey and salt to taste in a screw-top jar. Cover and shake well to mix.

3 Cut the cheese and ham into strips about 5 x 2 cm (2 x ¾ in). Place in a large salad bowl and add the beans, tomatoes, mushrooms, watercress, spinach and rocket. Toss together to combine evenly.

4 Just before serving, shake the dressing again and sprinkle it over the salad. Toss well, scatter over the chives and serve.

Some more ideas

- If you prefer, omit the ham and increase the cheese to 150 g (5½ oz).
- Fruits such as peaches work well with Gruyère, and could be added in thick slices to the salad in place of the tomatoes.
- For an Edam, apple and hazelnut salad, cut any rind from 200 g (7 oz) Edam cheese, then cut the cheese into small cubes. Mix in a bowl with 2 large carrots, cut into fine sticks, and 2 crisp eating apples, sliced and tossed in a little lemon juice to prevent browning. Add 170 g (6 oz) mixed wild rocket, frisée and mizuna or lamb's lettuce. For the dressing, shake 3 tbsp sunflower oil, 2 tbsp lemon juice, 1 tsp wholegrain mustard, 1 tsp clear honey, and salt and pepper to taste in a screw-top jar. Add to the salad and toss well. Scatter over 2–3 tbsp chopped parsley, 170 g (6 oz) diced cooked beetroot and 55 g (2 oz) chopped toasted hazelnuts. Toss again and serve.

Plus points

- Gruyère cheese is a good source of zinc. This mineral is essential for wound healing and enhances taste and flavour perception.
- The combination of green beans, tomatoes, watercress and salad leaves ensures a good intake of B vitamins and vitamins C and E.
- Ham is a good source of vitamin B_1, essential for the release of energy from carbohydrate foods such as bread.

Each serving provides

kcal 266, protein 16 g, fat 20 g (of which saturated fat 8 g), carbohydrate 7 g (of which sugars 6 g), fibre 3 g

✓✓✓	A, E, calcium
✓✓	C, copper, zinc
✓	B_1, B_2, B_6, B_{12}, folate, niacin, iron, potassium, selenium

for maximum vitality

Roquefort, pear and watercress salad

The ingredients of this fresh and vibrant salad, with contrasting colours, textures and flavours, are perfectly complemented by the subtle walnut oil dressing. The walnut flavour is strengthened by adding lightly toasted walnut pieces to the salad. Serve for a tempting lunch, accompanied by crusty wholegrain rolls or bread.

Serves 4

55 g (2 oz) walnut pieces

1 red onion, thinly sliced

3 large, ripe dessert pears, preferably red-skinned

115 g (4 oz) watercress

115 g (4 oz) Roquefort cheese, crumbled

pepper

Walnut and poppy seed dressing

½ tsp Dijon mustard

2 tsp red wine vinegar

1 tbsp sunflower oil

1 tbsp walnut oil

2 tsp poppy seeds

Preparation time: 15 minutes

Each serving provides ⓥ

kcal 348, **protein** 10 g, **fat** 26 g (of which saturated fat 7 g), **carbohydrate** 22 g (of which sugars 21 g), **fibre** 6 g

✓✓   A, C, E, calcium, copper

✓   B₁, B₂, B₆, niacin, iron, potassium, zinc

1 First make the dressing. Stir the mustard and vinegar together in a salad bowl with pepper to taste, then gradually whisk in the sunflower and walnuts oils. Stir in the poppy seeds. Set aside while preparing the salad.

2 Lightly toast the walnut pieces in a small frying pan, stirring them frequently. Leave to cool.

3 Add the red onion to the salad bowl and mix with the dressing. Quarter, core and slice the pears, leaving the skins on. Add to the bowl and toss gently to coat with the dressing.

4 Add the watercress and most of the cheese and walnuts to the pears. Toss together gently, then scatter over the remaining cheese and nuts, and serve immediately.

Some more ideas

● Other blue cheese, such as Stilton or Danish blue, works equally well here. As most blue cheeses are fairly salty, it isn't necessary to season the dressing with salt.

● For a ricotta and chicory salad, separate the leaves of 2 small heads of chicory, about 170 g (6 oz) in total. Cut each leaf in half lengthways and arrange on a serving platter. In a small jug, mix together 1 tsp Dijon mustard, 1 tbsp orange juice, ½ tsp finely grated orange zest, and salt and pepper to taste. Whisk in 1 tbsp sunflower oil and 1 tbsp walnut or hazelnut oil to make a creamy dressing. Cook 170 g (6 oz) sugarsnap peas in boiling water for about 3 minutes or until just tender, then drain and refresh under cold running water. Put into a mixing bowl and add 2 avocados, sliced horizontally into half moons, 4 plum tomatoes, cut into very thin wedges, and 75 g (2½ oz) toasted pecan nut halves. Drizzle over the dressing and toss gently to coat. Spoon on top of the chicory, dot spoonfuls of 200 g (7 oz) ricotta cheese over the surface, and serve.

Plus points

● Cheese contains valuable nutrients, so it is well worth including it in a well-balanced diet. Those cheeses that are high in fat, such as strongly flavoured Roquefort, need only be used in small quantities to contribute taste as well as their health benefits.

● Watercress is a good source of vitamin C, vitamin E and beta-carotene. It also contains a compound that has been shown to have antibiotic properties.

● When ripe, pears have a high natural sugar content. They are also a good source of potassium, which is needed to help regulate blood pressure.

Stuffed eggs en salade

The hollows in hard-boiled egg halves make perfect containers for a tasty filling – here carrot and chive – and the eggs look so pretty served on a bed of ribbon vegetables and lamb's lettuce. All you need is some interesting bread, such as pan gallego with sunflower, pumpkin and millet seeds, to make a satisfying lunch.

Serves 4

8 eggs, at room temperature

2 tbsp mayonnaise

2 tbsp plain low-fat yogurt

1 tsp mustard powder

100 g (3½ oz) carrot, finely grated

2 tbsp snipped fresh chives

Tarragon dressing

2 tbsp extra virgin olive oil

2 tsp tarragon vinegar

½ tsp Dijon mustard

salt and pepper

Orange and green salad

1 carrot

1 small bulb of fennel

2 courgettes

85 g (3 oz) lamb's lettuce

Preparation and cooking time: 25 minutes

Each serving provides Ⓥ

kcal 328, **protein** 18 g, **fat** 25 g (of which saturated fat 5 g), **carbohydrate** 8 g (of which sugars 7.5 g), **fibre** 3 g

✓✓✓	A, B$_{12}$
✓✓	B$_2$, E, folate, zinc
✓	B$_1$, B$_6$, C, niacin, calcium, copper, iron, potassium, selenium

1 First hard-boil the eggs. Place in a large saucepan, cover with tepid water and bring to the boil. Reduce the heat and simmer for 7 minutes. Remove the eggs with a draining spoon and place in a bowl of cold water to cool.

2 Meanwhile, make the dressing. Put the olive oil, vinegar and mustard in a screw-top jar with salt and pepper to taste. Shake well, then set aside.

3 Peel the eggs and cut each in half lengthways. Scoop out the yolks into a bowl using a teaspoon. Set the whites aside.

4 Add the mayonnaise, yogurt, mustard powder, grated carrot and half of the chives to the egg yolks, and mash together. Season with salt and pepper to taste. Using a teaspoon, spoon the egg yolk filling into the hollows in the egg white halves, mounding it up attractively.

5 Using a swivel vegetable peeler or a mandolin, shave thin ribbons lengthways from the carrot, fennel and courgettes. Put the vegetable ribbons in a mixing bowl with the lamb's lettuce. Shake the dressing again, then pour over the salad and toss together.

6 Divide the salad among 4 plates and top each with 4 stuffed egg halves. Sprinkle the top of the eggs with the remaining chives, and serve.

Some more ideas

● For a lightly curried filling, mix the egg yolks with 4 tbsp reduced-fat soft cheese, 1½ tsp curry paste, 2 finely chopped spring onions and the grated carrot.

● Add 3–4 finely chopped radishes to the stuffing mixture.

Plus points

● Eggs have often been given a 'bad press' because of their cholesterol content. In fact, for most people, eating eggs and other foods rich in cholesterol has little detrimental effect on blood cholesterol levels.

● Preparing vegetables just before use helps to minimise vitamin loss.

● By mixing mayonnaise with yogurt. rather than using mayonnaise alone, the fat and calorie contents of a dish such as this can be reduced.

Feta and couscous salad

Apart from being an excellent source of starchy carbohydrate, couscous is a great background for other ingredients. In this lunch salad, both raw and lightly steamed vegetables are added to the couscous together with toasted almonds, fresh mint and creamy feta cheese. A touch of chilli gives extra bite to the dressing.

Serves 4

225 g (8 oz) couscous
300 ml (10 fl oz) hot vegetable stock
170 g (6 oz) slim asparagus spears, halved
2 courgettes, cut into thin sticks
1 red pepper, seeded and cut into thin strips
30 g (1 oz) toasted flaked almonds
handful of fresh mint leaves, finely chopped
170 g (6 oz) feta cheese

Chilli dressing

3 tbsp extra virgin olive oil
grated zest of 1 lemon
1 tbsp lemon juice
1 garlic clove, finely chopped
½ tsp crushed dried chillies
salt and pepper

Preparation and cooking time: 30–35 minutes

Each serving provides

(V)

kcal 388, protein 14 g, fat 22 g (of which saturated fat 7.5 g), carbohydrate 35 g (of which sugars 5 g), fibre 2 g

✓✓✓	A, C
✓✓	E, folate, calcium, iron
✓	B₁, B₆, B₁₂, niacin, copper, potassium, zinc

1 Put the couscous into a large bowl and pour over the hot stock. Set aside to soak for 15–20 minutes or until all the liquid has been absorbed.

2 Meanwhile, steam the asparagus for 3 minutes. Add the courgettes and continue steaming for 2 minutes or until the vegetables are just tender but still retain some crunch. Tip the vegetables into a colander and refresh under cold running water. Drain well.

3 To make the dressing, combine the oil, lemon zest and juice, garlic, chillies, and salt and pepper to taste in a screw-top jar. Shake well to blend.

4 Fluff up the couscous with a fork, then fold in the pepper strips, almonds, mint, and steamed asparagus and courgettes. Pour over the dressing and stir gently together. Crumble the feta over the top, and serve.

Some more ideas

- If you can get yellow courgettes, use 1 yellow and 1 green for even more colour.
- Instead of, or as well as, mint, use other herbs such as chopped fresh coriander.
- For a halloumi and lentil salad, cook 85 g (3 oz) Puy lentils in plenty of boiling water for 15–20 minutes or until just tender. At the same time, cook 115 g (4 oz) long-grain rice in boiling water for 10–15 minutes, or according to the packet instructions, until tender. Add 170 g (6 oz) broad beans or peas (fresh or frozen) to the lentils for the last 4 minutes of the cooking time. Drain the rice and lentils well, then mix them together. Stir in 3 finely chopped spring onions, 1 red pepper, seeded and diced, and 30 g (1 oz) toasted flaked almonds. Make the chilli dressing as in the main recipe, and toss with the rice and lentil salad. Cut 170 g (6 oz) halloumi cheese into 8 slices. Brush each slice with a little extra virgin olive oil, using about 1 tbsp oil in all, then grill or griddle for a few minutes or until golden on both sides. Serve the salad topped with the cheese and an extra grinding of black pepper.

Plus points

- Feta cheese is quite salty. If you are concerned about your sodium intake you can reduce the salt content of the cheese by soaking it in milk for 30 minutes before use (discard the milk).
- Couscous, made from semolina, is low in fat and high in starchy carbohydrate.
- Courgettes belong to the same family as melons, cucumbers and pumpkins. Their skin is a rich source of beta-carotene, which the body can convert into vitamin A. This vitamin helps to maintain healthy eyesight and skin, and a properly functioning immune system.

Garlicky fresh cheese

This tangy, soft-textured yogurt cheese, flavoured with herbs and garlic, makes a healthy starter or snack, and is a great addition to a picnic basket, too. The garlic is blanched for a sweeter flavour. Serve with fresh vegetables for dipping, plus wholemeal bread, such as soda bread, to be spread with the cheese.

Serves 4

150 g (5½ oz) plain low-fat bio yogurt
150 g (5½ oz) fromage frais
2 large garlic cloves
1 tbsp snipped fresh chives
1 tbsp chopped parsley
2 tsp chopped fresh dill
1 tsp finely grated lemon zest
salt and pepper

To serve

1 head chicory, leaves separated
4 carrots, cut into 5 cm (2 in) sticks
1 bunch spring onions
4 celery sticks, cut into 5 cm (2 in) sticks
4 slices wholemeal soda bread, about 170 g
  (6 oz) in total, cut into large chunks

Preparation and cooking time: 30–35 minutes, plus overnight draining

Each serving provides Ⓥ

kcal 229, **protein** 10 g, **fat** 5 g (of which saturated fat 2 g), **carbohydrate** 40 g (of which sugars 15 g), **fibre** 5 g

✓✓✓	A
✓✓	C, calcium
✓	B₁, B₂, B₆, B₁₂, folate, niacin, copper, iron, potassium, zinc

1 Line a deep sieve with a double thickness of muslin and set over a bowl. Mix together the yogurt and fromage frais until smooth, then spoon into the muslin-lined sieve. Wrap the muslin over the top and put into the refrigerator. Leave to drain overnight.

2 The next day, drop the unpeeled garlic cloves into a small pan of boiling water and simmer for 3 minutes or until soft. Drain. Squeeze the garlic flesh out of the skins and mash or chop.

3 Unwrap the drained yogurt mixture and put it into a clean bowl (discard the liquid that has drained from the mixture). Add the blanched garlic, herbs and lemon zest to the yogurt cheese, and season with salt and pepper to taste. (The yogurt cheese can be kept, covered, in the fridge for 3–4 days.)

4 Spoon the yogurt cheese into a small bowl and set on a platter. Arrange the prepared vegetables and bread chunks around, and serve.

Some more ideas

● Thoroughly chill the yogurt cheese, then form it into a small 'barrel' shape. Roll in 75 g (2½ oz) finely chopped walnuts or hazelnuts to coat on all sides.

● For an olive and caper cheese, mash 45 g (1½ oz) feta cheese and stir into the freshly drained yogurt cheese together with ½ tsp crushed dried chillies, 1 crushed garlic clove, 1 tbsp chopped capers, 1 tbsp chopped black olives, 1 tbsp chopped fresh oregano and seasoning to taste. Serve as a starter or snack for 6, with the crudités and toasted pitta bread.

Plus points

● This home-made soft cheese is much lower in fat than similar commercial cheeses, yet it is just as tasty. There is no need to add salt to the mixture as the herbs, garlic and lemon provide lots of flavour.

● Recently published research suggests that garlic has a role to play in reducing blood cholesterol levels and inhibiting blood clotting. Including garlic in the diet on a regular basis may therefore help to reduce the risk of heart disease and stroke.

Mozzarella with grilled fennel and peppers on crostini

Here is a colourful, Mediterranean-style dish that is very easy to make. The vegetables can be prepared in advance if you like, and left to soak up the flavours in the dressing, then mixed with the mozzarella and piled onto freshly toasted, garlicky ciabatta bread. A perfect summer lunch.

Serves 4

1 large bulb of fennel, about 300 g (10½ oz)
3 tbsp extra virgin olive oil
1 small red onion, halved
1 red pepper, halved and seeded
1 yellow pepper, halved and seeded
2 tsp balsamic vinegar
150 g (5½ oz) mozzarella cheese, diced
85 g (3 oz) mixed salad leaves
15 g (½ oz) fresh basil leaves
1 ciabatta loaf, thickly sliced
1 garlic clove, halved
salt and pepper

Preparation and cooking time: about 45 minutes

Each serving provides Ⓥ

kcal 410, **protein** 19 g, **fat** 19 g (of which saturated fat 7 g), **carbohydrate** 42 g (of which sugars 8 g), **fibre** 5 g

✓✓✓	A, C
✓✓	B_{12}, calcium, selenium
✓	B_1, B_6, E, folate, niacin, copper, iron, potassium, zinc

1 Preheat the grill to high. Cut the fennel bulb in half lengthways, then cut each half lengthways into 1 cm (½ in) thick slices, not cutting all the way through the base so the layers remain attached. Place the halves cut side down on a baking tray and brush lightly with 1 tbsp of the oil.

2 Put the onion halves and peppers cut side down on the baking tray. Grill the vegetables for 10–15 minutes, turning once, until the fennel is golden brown and the peppers and onions are tender and blackened in places.

3 Transfer the vegetables to a chopping board (leave the grill on). Pour any juices from the baking tray into a small bowl and whisk in the remaining 2 tbsp oil and the balsamic vinegar. Season this dressing with salt and pepper to taste.

4 Thickly slice the peppers and onion. Cut through the base of the fennel halves to separate the slices. Put all the vegetables in a mixing bowl. Pour over the dressing and toss well to coat the vegetables evenly. Add the mozzarella, salad leaves and basil to the bowl, piling them on top of the vegetables (do not toss together yet).

5 Spread out the ciabatta slices on a clean baking sheet and toast under the grill for 2–3 minutes or until golden on both sides. Rub one side of each slice with the cut surface of the garlic clove; discard the garlic.

6 Toss the mozzarella, leaves and vegetables to mix them together, then pile on top of the ciabatta toasts. Serve immediately.

Plus points

- Mozzarella cheese is lower in fat than many other varieties of cheeses and so contains fewer calories.
- Fennel is believed to help digestion, particularly by relieving colic, stomach cramps and wind.
- Peppers are an excellent source of vitamin C and of beta-carotene. However, the beta-carotene content varies according to the colour of the pepper, red peppers having the most and green peppers the least.

for maximum vitality

Some more ideas

- For a rich, nutty flavour, replace the olive oil with hazelnut or walnut oil.
- To make mozzarella and vegetable pitta pockets, cut 4 pitta breads across in half and warm under the grill. Open the pockets and spoon in the mozzarella and grilled vegetables.
- Make the classic Italian mozzarella, avocado and tomato salad and serve on toasted ciabatta. Peel a large avocado and cut across into slices. Slice 2 large, ripe tomatoes and 150 g (5½ oz) mozzarella. Mix together 2 tbsp extra virgin olive oil, 2 tsp balsamic vinegar, and seasoning to taste in a bowl. Add the avocado, tomatoes and mozzarella, together with a handful of torn fresh basil leaves, and mix gently with the dressing. Toast the ciabatta and rub with garlic as in the main recipe, then top with the salad and serve.

67

Quail's eggs with asparagus and Parmesan shavings

Make this lovely, warm salad in late spring with the new season's asparagus. The lightly steamed, bright green spears are topped with poached quail's eggs, then finished with Parmesan shavings and a salad of lamb's lettuce and crunchy chicory. Accompany with slices of crisp baguette for an easy lunch.

Serves 4

125 g (4½ oz) lamb's lettuce

2 heads chicory, about 170 g (6 oz) in total

15 g (½ oz) fresh chives, snipped

750 g (1 lb 10 oz) asparagus

1 tsp vinegar

12 quail's eggs

50 g (1¾ oz) Parmesan cheese, cut into fine shavings

Mustard vinaigrette

2 tbsp extra virgin olive oil

2 tsp red wine vinegar

1 garlic clove, crushed

½ tsp wholegrain mustard

salt and pepper

Preparation and cooking time: about 25 minutes

Each serving provides

kcal 233, **protein** 17 g, **fat** 16 g (of which saturated fat 5 g), **carbohydrate** 6 g (of which sugars 5 g), **fibre** 4 g

✓✓✓	folate
✓✓	A, B₁, C, E, calcium, zinc
✓	B₂, B₆, niacin, copper, iron, potassium

1 Break up any large bunches of lamb's lettuce, then put into a mixing bowl. Thinly slice the chicory on the diagonal, discarding the last 1 cm (½ in) of the base. Add to the lamb's lettuce together with the chives and toss together. Set aside.

2 Put all the ingredients for the dressing in a screw-top jar and season with salt and pepper to taste. Shake together to mix.

3 Steam the asparagus for about 4 minutes or until barely tender. Alternatively, cook the asparagus in a wide pan of simmering water for 3–4 minutes. To test, pierce the thickest part of the stalk with a thin, sharp knife. If cooked in simmering water, carefully lift out the asparagus spears with a draining spoon and drain thoroughly on kitchen paper.

4 While the asparagus is cooking, half fill a frying pan with water and bring to the boil. Add the vinegar, then reduce the heat so the water is just simmering. Carefully crack 4 of the quail's eggs, one at a time, and slip into the water. Cook for 1 minute or until the yolks have just set. Remove the poached eggs from the water with a draining spoon and drain on kitchen paper. Keep warm while poaching the rest of the quail's eggs.

5 Pour the dressing over the salad and toss together. Spread out on a large serving platter. Arrange the asparagus on the salad and place the poached eggs on top. Scatter over the Parmesan shavings and grind a little pepper over the top. Serve immediately.

Plus points

- Though much smaller in size, quail's eggs have a very similar nutritional composition to hen's eggs. They therefore contain useful amounts of protein, plus vitamins A, E, B₂, B₁₂ and niacin.
- Asparagus is a good source of many of the B vitamins, including folate which is important during the early stages of pregnancy, to prevent birth defects such as spina bifida.
- Parmesan cheese has a higher content of vitamin B₁₂ than other cheeses. This vitamin is important for the formation of red blood cells and for helping to keep the nervous system healthy.

Some more ideas

● Use rocket instead of chicory.

● For quail's eggs with new potatoes and spinach, cook 500 g (1 lb 2 oz) scrubbed new potatoes in boiling water for about 15 minutes or until tender; drain and cut in half. While the potatoes are cooking, grill 4 rashers of lean back bacon until crisp, then drain on kitchen paper and crumble. Toss the warm potatoes and bacon with 300 g (10½ oz) baby spinach leaves and 1 small red onion, finely chopped. Keep warm. Poach 12 quail's eggs as in the main recipe. Set the eggs on top of the spinach and potato salad, season with a grinding of pepper and serve immediately.

Quick Egg and Dairy Dishes

In 30 minutes or less

Eggs and dairy products are ideal fast food ingredients easily transformed into all kinds of delicious and nutritious meals in minutes. Pasta is a popular quick staple, and works well with most cheeses, not just Parmesan. Try it with softly melting Brie, plus cherry tomatoes, asparagus and basil, or tossed with a creamy goat's cheese, olive and caper sauce. Make a toasted sandwich filled with mozzarella and sun-dried tomatoes. Turn eggs into omelettes or cook them in a rich vegetable stew. Or sauté ginger-marinated feta with prawns.

Spaghetti with Brie and cherry tomatoes

Here is a colourful pasta dish full of fresh summery flavours. The asparagus and tomatoes are very lightly cooked before tossing with the hot pasta and cubes of Brie – the tomatoes gently burst and release their sweet juices, and the heat makes the cheese just start to melt.

Serves 4

400 g (14 oz) spaghetti

2 tbsp extra virgin olive oil

2 plump garlic cloves, finely chopped

170 g (6 oz) thin asparagus, cut into 5 cm (2 in) pieces

300 g (10½ oz) cherry tomatoes, halved

large handful of fresh basil leaves, roughly torn

170 g (6 oz) Brie cheese, cut into cubes

salt and pepper

Preparation and cooking time: 30 minutes

1 Cook the pasta in a large pan of boiling water for 10–12 minutes, or according to the packet instructions, until al dente.

2 Meanwhile, heat the oil in a large frying pan, add the garlic and cook for about 30 seconds. Don't let it brown. Tip in the asparagus and add 4 tbsp of water. Cook over a moderate heat for 3–5 minutes, stirring frequently, until the asparagus is just tender and most of the water has evaporated.

3 Add the cherry tomatoes and basil, and cook for a further 2 minutes or until the tomatoes start to soften but still hold their shape. Season with salt and pepper to taste.

4 Drain the pasta in a colander, then pour it into a large serving bowl. Add the vegetable mixture and the Brie, and toss gently to mix. Serve hot, sprinkled with a grinding of pepper.

Some more ideas

● Replace the Brie with Camembert.

● For spaghetti with Brie, asparagus and fresh tomato salsa, cook the pasta as in the main recipe, adding the asparagus to the pan for the last 3 minutes of the cooking time. Meanwhile, finely chop 300 g (10½ oz) ripe tomatoes and mix with 1 finely chopped small red onion, 4 tbsp chopped parsley, 1 crushed garlic clove, 2 tbsp extra virgin olive oil, and salt and pepper to taste. Drain the pasta and asparagus, and tip them into a large serving bowl. Add the salsa and the cheese, and toss gently to mix.

● Make rigatoni with mozzarella and rocket. Replace the spaghetti with rigatoni (or penne), and the Brie with 150 g (5½ oz) mozzarella. Omit the asparagus and water, and increase the quantity of tomatoes to 500 g (1 lb 2 oz). In step 4, add 100 g (3½ oz) rocket with the mozzarella, tossing with the pasta just until the leaves wilt and the cheese begins to melt.

Plus points

● Cheese and tomatoes are a traditional combination, and together they provide protein and many essential vitamins and minerals.

● Brie is made from full-fat cow's milk, but because it has a high water content it contains less fat than hard, dense cheeses such as Cheddar.

● Basil, a member of the mint family, is believed to aid digestion and relieve the headaches that often occur with a cold.

Each serving provides Ⓥ

kcal 553, **protein** 22 g, **fat** 19 g (of which saturated fat 8 g), **carbohydrate** 77 g (of which sugars 6 g), **fibre** 4 g

✓✓ A, C, folate, niacin, calcium, copper, zinc

✓ B₁, B₂, B₆, B₁₂, E, iron, potassium

Golden penne with goat's cheese

Mild and creamy goat's cheese is melted in saffron-infused white wine and mixed with fennel, olives and capers to make a golden-coloured sauce for pasta shapes. This easy dish comes with a simple mixed leaf salad.

Serves 4

large pinch of saffron threads

100 ml (3½ fl oz) dry white wine

400 g (14 oz) penne or other pasta shapes

30 g (1 oz) pine nuts

1 tbsp extra virgin olive oil

1 bulb of fennel, very thinly sliced

2 garlic cloves, crushed

55 g (2 oz) stoned black olives, roughly chopped

1 tbsp capers, drained

1 tbsp chopped fresh marjoram

170 g (6 oz) soft goat's cheese

salt and pepper

sprigs of fresh marjoram to garnish

Mixed leaf salad

1 tbsp sunflower oil

1 tbsp orange juice

1 tsp sherry vinegar

170 g (6 oz) assorted salad leaves such as Oak Leaf, rocket, Lollo Rosso and watercress

Preparation and cooking time: 30 minutes

Each serving provides ⓥ

kcal 584, **protein** 20 g, **fat** 21 g (of which saturated fat 6 g), **carbohydrate** 80 g (of which sugars 5 g), **fibre** 6 g

✓✓	A, B$_{12}$, E, niacin, copper, selenium, zinc
✓	B$_1$, B$_2$, folate, calcium, iron, potassium

1 Crumble the saffron threads into a small mixing bowl. Heat the wine in a large, non-stick frying pan until steaming hot, then pour it over the saffron. Leave to infuse. Wipe out the frying pan with kitchen paper and set it aside.

2 For the salad, combine the oil, orange juice and vinegar in a salad bowl. Season with salt and pepper to taste, and whisk to mix. Pile the salad leaves on top of the dressing, but do not toss. Set aside.

3 Cook the pasta in a large pan of boiling water for 10–12 minutes, or according to the packet instructions, until al dente.

4 Meanwhile, toast the pine nuts in the frying pan over a moderately high heat for 2–3 minutes, stirring constantly, until golden. Tip the pine nuts into a bowl and set aside.

5 Heat the oil in the frying pan over a moderate heat and cook the sliced fennel for 5–6 minutes or until soft. Add the garlic and cook for a further minute, stirring well. Stir in the olives, capers and chopped marjoram.

6 Add the goat's cheese and the saffron-infused wine. Season with salt and pepper to taste, and heat gently, stirring occasionally, until the cheese has melted smoothly into the liquid to make a sauce.

7 Drain the pasta in a colander, then tip it into the frying pan. Gently toss to coat the pasta with the sauce. Spoon onto warmed serving plates, sprinkle with the toasted pine nuts and garnish with sprigs of fresh marjoram. Serve immediately, with the quickly tossed salad.

Plus points

● Cheese made from goat's milk provides protein, calcium and phosphorus plus several B vitamins.

● Pasta is an excellent source of starchy carbohydrate and it is low in fat, so fits well into the recommendations for healthy eating.

● Pine nuts are a good source of vitamin E. This important antioxidant helps the body to fight harmful free radicals that can damage cells and cause illness and disease.

Another idea

• Make pasta with sautéed butternut squash and fontina. Cut 400 g (14 oz) peeled and seeded butternut squash into 1 cm (½ in) cubes. Heat 15 g (½ oz) butter with 1 tsp extra virgin olive oil in a large frying pan, add the squash and sauté over a moderate heat for 8–10 minutes or until lightly browned and tender. Meanwhile, cook 400 g (14 oz) pasta shapes such as orecchiette (little ears) or conchiglie (shells) in boiling water for 10–12 minutes, or according to packet instructions, until al dente. Add 1 crushed garlic clove to the squash and cook for a further 30 seconds.

Drain the pasta and add to the squash in the frying pan, together with 125 g (4½ oz) fontina or taleggio cheese, cut into 1 cm (½ in) cubes, 55 g (2 oz) Parma ham, trimmed of all fat and cut into thin strips, and 2 tbsp chopped parsley. Toss gently to mix. Serve with the mixed leaf salad in the main recipe.

Mozzarella in carrozza

This classic Italian sandwich, which literally means 'mozzarella in a carriage', makes a delicious and very quick vegetarian meal. Chopped sun-dried tomatoes and fresh basil leaves enhance the flavour of the cheese, which melts on cooking to a wonderful oozing texture in the middle of the eggy bread.

Serves 4

8 slices close-textured white bread, cut
   1 cm (½ in) thick, about 325 g (11½ oz)
   in total

170 g (6 oz) mozzarella cheese, grated

85 g (3 oz) sun-dried tomatoes packed in oil,
   well drained and roughly chopped

16 large fresh basil leaves

150 ml (5 fl oz) semi-skimmed milk

2 large eggs, beaten

1 tbsp extra virgin olive oil

salt and pepper

Tomato and orange salad

2 oranges

6 plum tomatoes, sliced

1 tsp balsamic vinegar

1 garlic clove, crushed

30 g (1 oz) stoned black olives, halved

Preparation time: 15 minutes
Cooking time: 8–10 minutes

Each serving provides Ⓥ

kcal 570, **protein** 26 g, **fat** 30 g (of which saturated fat 9 g), **carbohydrate** 54 g (of which sugars 15 g), **fibre** 4 g

✓✓✓	A, B₁₂, C, E, calcium
✓✓	B₁, folate, niacin, copper, selenium, zinc
✓	B₂, B₆, iron, potassium

1 First make the salad. Peel and slice the oranges, working over a bowl to catch all the juice. Arrange the tomatoes and orange slices, slightly overlapping, in a shallow dish. Add the vinegar, garlic, and salt and pepper to taste to the orange juice and whisk to mix. Sprinkle this dressing over the salad. Scatter over the olives. Set aside.

2 Lay 4 of the slices of bread on a board or work surface. Divide the mozzarella cheese evenly among the slices. Scatter the sun-dried tomatoes on the cheese, then arrange the basil leaves over the tomatoes. Place the remaining 4 slices of bread on top and press down firmly.

3 Pour the milk into a shallow bowl. Add the eggs and season with salt and pepper to taste. Gently whisk together. Lay the sandwiches in the bowl, one at a time, and spoon the milk and egg mixture over so that the bread on both sides is evenly and thoroughly moistened.

4 Lightly grease a ridged cast-iron grill pan or griddle with 1½ tsp of the oil. Heat the pan over a moderate heat. Place 2 of the sandwiches in the pan and cook for 1–2 minutes on each side, turning carefully with 2 spatulas to hold the sandwiches together, until golden brown and crisp.

5 Remove the sandwiches from the pan and keep warm while cooking the other 2 sandwiches, using the remaining 1½ tsp oil. Cut the sandwiches in half and serve hot, with the tomato and orange salad.

Plus points

● Mozzarella melts beautifully and has a mild flavour, so makes a toasted sandwich that is sure to be popular with children. Unlike other lower-fat cheeses, mozzarella is an excellent source of calcium.

● Bread has often been considered to be a 'fattening' food, but in fact it is what is normally put on the bread that may be fattening. White bread provides good amounts of dietary fibre, B vitamins and calcium.

● Tomatoes ripened in the sun can contain up to 4 times as much vitamin C as those ripened in a greenhouse, and using them raw is the best way to benefit from their vitamin C content.

Some more ideas

● Use anchovies instead of sun-dried tomatoes. Drain 1 can of anchovies, about 50 g, mash and spread over the 4 slices of bread before adding the mozzarella.

● To make croque-monsieur, spread 1 tsp of wholegrain mustard on each of 4 thick slices of white or wholemeal bread. Scatter 25 g (scant 1 oz) grated Gruyère cheese on top of each slice, then add a 20 g (¾ oz) slice of smoked ham, trimmed of all fat. Cover with 4 more slices of bread and press together. Brush the top of each sandwich with ½ tsp extra virgin olive oil. Toast for 1 minute under a preheated hot grill, then carefully turn the sandwiches over. Brush the other sides with olive oil as before and grill until crisp and golden. Serve hot with a frisée and radicchio salad. To make the salad, toss 100 g (3½ oz) each roughly torn frisée and radicchio with ½ cucumber, sliced. Add a garlic vinaigrette dressing made with 1 tbsp extra virgin olive oil, 1 tsp red wine vinegar, 1 tsp clear honey, 1 tsp Dijon mustard, 1 crushed garlic clove and seasoning to taste.

Ricotta bruschetta

With a selection of Italian-style antipasto vegetables in your storecupboard, interesting light meals and snacks can be prepared in minutes, such as these tasty toasts topped with peppers and ricotta cheese. A salad of mixed leaves with cucumber and grapes is all that's needed to make a sustaining lunch.

Serves 4

8 slices of sourdough bread, cut 1 cm (½ in) thick, about 300 g (10½ oz) in total

250 g (8½ oz) ricotta cheese

55 g (2 oz) stoned green olives, chopped

3 tbsp chopped fresh mint

150 g (5½ oz) antipasto peppers, well drained and roughly chopped

salt and pepper

fresh mint leaves to garnish

Leaf and grape salad

2 tbsp extra virgin olive oil

1 tsp lemon juice

170 g (6 oz) mixed salad leaves, such as baby spinach, Oak Leaf and rocket

½ cucumber, sliced

225 g (8 oz) seedless red or green grapes

Preparation and cooking time: about 25 minutes

Each serving provides   Ⓥ

kcal 408, **protein** 13 g, **fat** 16 g (of which saturated fat 5 g), **carbohydrate** 55 g (of which sugars 16 g), **fibre** 4 g

✓✓✓	A
✓✓	C, calcium
✓	B₁, B₆, E, folate, niacin, copper, iron, potassium, zinc

1 First make the salad dressing. Put the olive oil, lemon juice, and salt and pepper to taste in a salad bowl and whisk to mix. Set the bowl aside.

2 Heat a large, ridged, cast-iron grill pan over a moderately high heat. Put in as many slices of bread as will fit in a single layer and toast them for about 2 minutes or until the bases are crisp and lightly marked with ridges. Turn the slices over and toast on the other side. Remove the slices. Toast the remaining slices in the same way.

3 Put the ricotta cheese in a mixing bowl and add the olives and chopped mint. Season with salt and pepper to taste. Mix well together.

4 Place a few pepper pieces on each slice of toast. Pile the ricotta mixture on top and garnish with mint leaves.

5 Quickly whisk the dressing in the salad bowl, then add the salad leaves, sliced cucumber and grapes. Toss together, and serve with the bruschetta.

Another idea

● Make a taleggio, tuna and mushroom topping for focaccia bread. Drain 1 can of tuna in spring water, about 200 g, and flake into a bowl. Add 100 g (3½ oz) well drained mixed antipasto peppers in oil, 100 g (3½ oz) well drained mixed antipasto mushrooms in oil and 2 tbsp chopped parsley. Season with salt and pepper to taste. Stir together until well blended. Cut 6 thick slices of focaccia bread, about 300 g (10½ oz) in total, then slice each in half horizontally. Toast the bread under a preheated hot grill for about 2 minutes on each side or until crisp. Spread the tuna mixture over the toasts, then top with 150 g (5½ oz) taleggio cheese, thinly sliced. Grill for 2½ minutes or until the cheese melts. Serve hot.

Plus points

● Ricotta is an Italian cheese made from the whey left over from making other cheeses. It is similar to fromage frais in nutritional composition, although it has a higher protein and calcium content.

● Olive oil is high in monounsaturated fat, which is thought to help in lowering high levels of cholesterol in the blood.

Sweetcorn fritters

In this recipe, crisp, juicy sweetcorn kernels are added to a thick batter flavoured with chilli and fresh coriander, and then pan-fried in big spoonfuls. Piled on a bed of watercress and drizzled with a minted spring onion and yogurt sauce, the fritters make a delicious quick meal.

Serves 4 (makes 12 fritters)

140 g (5 oz) plain flour

½ tsp baking powder

150 ml (5 fl oz) semi-skimmed milk

2 large eggs, lightly beaten

400 g (14 oz) frozen sweetcorn kernels, thawed and drained

3 spring onions, finely chopped

1 fat fresh red chilli, seeded and finely chopped

3 heaped tbsp chopped fresh coriander

1 tbsp sunflower oil

115 g (4 oz) watercress

salt and pepper

Yogurt sauce

300 g (10½ oz) Greek-style yogurt

4 spring onions, finely chopped

2 tbsp chopped fresh mint

grated zest and juice of 1 lime

Preparation and cooking time: 30 minutes

Each serving provides
kcal 394, **protein** 17 g, **fat** 15 g (of which saturated fat 6 g), **carbohydrate** 51 g (of which sugars 9 g), **fibre** 3 g

✓✓✓	A, C
✓✓	B₁, B₂, B₁₂, E, calcium, zinc
✓	B₆, folate, niacin, copper, iron, potassium, selenium

1 First make the yogurt sauce. Put the yogurt into a serving bowl and stir in the spring onions, mint, lime zest and a pinch of salt. Cover and chill while you make the fritters (keep the lime juice for use later).

2 Sift the flour and baking powder into a bowl. Make a well in the centre and add the milk and eggs. Using a wooden spoon, mix together the milk and eggs, then gradually draw in the flour from around the edges. Beat with the spoon to make a smooth, thick batter. Alternatively, the batter can be made in a food processor: put the milk and egg in the container first, spoon the flour and baking powder on top, and process for a few seconds to blend.

3 Add the sweetcorn kernels, spring onions, chilli and coriander to the batter, and season with salt and pepper to taste. Mix well.

4 Heat a griddle or large, heavy frying pan, then brush with a little of the oil. Drop large spoonfuls of the fritter batter onto the pan – make about 4 fritters at a time – and cook over a moderate heat for 2 minutes or until golden and firm on the underside.

5 Turn the fritters over using a palette knife, and cook on the other side for about 2 minutes or until golden brown. Remove the fritters from the pan and drain on kitchen paper. Keep warm while cooking the rest of the fritters in the same way, adding more oil to the pan as necessary.

6 Arrange the watercress on 4 plates and sprinkle with the lime juice. Arrange the sweetcorn fritters on top and serve hot, with the yogurt sauce to be drizzled over.

Plus points
● Sweetcorn is a useful source of fibre as well as vitamins A, C and folate. It is generally a popular food with children and this recipe makes a healthy dish they are sure to love.

● In the past, those at risk of heart disease or stroke have been advised to limit their intake of eggs to 2 a week. Recent research now suggests that unless you suffer from diabetes, you can safely eat up to 7 eggs a week.

● Watercress, like other dark green, leafy vegetables, contains folate, a B vitamin, which recent research suggests may help to protect the body against heart disease and prevent Alzheimer's disease.

quick egg and dairy dishes

Some more ideas

- Instead of chilli and coriander, flavour the batter with 2 tsp green Thai curry paste.
- Make pea fritters by replacing the sweetcorn with frozen peas. Use chopped fresh basil in place of coriander.
- For Indian-style spicy vegetable fritters, make a batter with 140 g (5 oz) gram (chickpea) flour, ½ tsp baking powder, 120 ml (4 fl oz) semi-skimmed milk and 1 egg. Flavour the batter with 3 tbsp chopped fresh coriander, 1 tbsp chopped fresh root ginger, 1 tsp turmeric, 1 tsp cumin seeds, ½ tsp chilli powder, 1 crushed garlic clove and ½ tsp salt. Rinse 150 g (5½ oz) spinach, then cook gently for about 2 minutes, with just the water clinging to the leaves; drain thoroughly and chop. Add to the batter together with 1 small, finely chopped onion, 1 coarsely grated courgette and 30 g (1 oz) pumpkin seeds. Cook the fritters as in the main recipe. Serve with a tomato and yogurt sauce, made by mixing 300 g (10½ oz) plain low-fat yogurt with 4 tbsp tomato passata and 3 tbsp chopped fresh coriander.

Cauliflower cheese soup

A classic combination as a vegetable dish, cauliflower and Cheddar cheese are equally good partners in a soup. Here the cauliflower is gently simmered in milk and stock, then puréed to a velvety-smooth texture. This is a warming soup that makes a simple lunch or supper dish, served with crusty rolls.

Serves 4

15 g (½ oz) butter

1 onion, chopped

¼ tsp mustard powder

1 large cauliflower, about 900 g (2 lb), broken into small florets

600 ml (1 pint) semi-skimmed milk

150 ml (5 fl oz) vegetable stock

1 bay leaf

2 tsp sunflower oil

100 g (3½ oz) mature Cheddar cheese, grated

salt and pepper

chopped fresh flat-leaf parsley to garnish

Preparation and cooking time: 30 minutes

1 Melt the butter in a large saucepan. Add the onion and cook over a moderate heat for 3 minutes, stirring frequently, until soft. Sprinkle over the mustard and stir it in.

2 Reserve about 85 g (3 oz) of the cauliflower florets; add the rest to the saucepan together with the milk, stock and bay leaf. Bring to the boil, then reduce the heat. Cover and simmer for 10 minutes or until the cauliflower is tender.

3 Meanwhile, heat the oil in a non-stick frying pan. Break the reserved cauliflower into tiny florets and fry for 4–5 minutes or until lightly browned, stirring frequently. Set aside.

4 Remove the bay leaf from the soup. Purée in the pan with a hand-held blender, or in a blender or food processor. Season with salt and pepper to taste, then reheat until just bubbling.

5 Remove from the heat, add the grated cheese and stir until melted. Ladle into warmed soup bowls and sprinkle with the sautéed cauliflower florets and parsley. Serve immediately.

Plus points

● Cheddar cheese, like most other cheeses, is a good source of protein and an excellent source of calcium, but it is high in fat. Reducing the amount of cheese that would normally be used in a dish like this, and choosing a mature cheese with a strong taste, keeps fat levels healthy, and the cheese still makes a valuable nutritional contribution.

● Cauliflower is a member of the brassica family of cruciferous vegetables. Its distinctive sulphurous compounds are believed to play a part in protecting against certain forms of cancer and heart disease.

● Onions are not only believed to help reduce the risk of cancer but also to help lower blood cholesterol levels.

Each serving provides   Ⓥ

kcal 303, **protein** 20 g, **fat** 18 g (of which saturated fat 10 g), **carbohydrate** 17 g (of which sugars 15 g), **fibre** 5 g

✓✓✓	C, calcium
✓✓	A, B₁, B₆, B₁₂, folate, potassium, zinc
✓	B₂, E, niacin, iron

Some more ideas

- Use all the cauliflower in the soup. For the garnish, mix together 4 tbsp plain low-fat yogurt and 2 tbsp chopped parsley or snipped fresh chives. Swirl a spoonful of this herb yogurt on top of each bowl of soup.
- For a spiced parsnip and cheese soup to serve 6, soften 1 finely chopped onion in 15 g (½ oz) butter. Stir in 550 g (1¼ lb) finely diced parsnips, 1 tsp cumin seeds and ½ tsp ground coriander. Cook for 2 minutes, then add 600 ml (1 pint) semi-skimmed milk, 450 ml (15 fl oz) vegetable stock and a bay leaf. Bring to the boil, then cover and simmer for 10 minutes or until the parsnips are tender. Remove the bay leaf and purée the soup with a hand-held blender, or in a blender or food processor. Reheat until piping hot. Ladle into warmed bowls and sprinkle with 115 g (4 oz) grated Red Leicester or Double Gloucester cheese. Garnish with a few torn fresh coriander leaves and serve hot.

Chakchouka

This dish is popular all over the Mediterranean region and there are many different variations. Basically it is a tomato-based vegetable stew, like a ratatouille, with eggs poached right in the mixture. Serve it for a fast and sustaining lunch for 2 with garlic and rosemary focaccia or olive ciabatta, or as a snack for 4.

Serves 2

1 tbsp extra virgin olive oil

1 small onion, roughly chopped

2 garlic cloves, crushed

1 red pepper, seeded and thinly sliced

1 green pepper, seeded and thinly sliced

400 g (14 oz) large ripe tomatoes, roughly chopped

2 tbsp tomato purée

¼ tsp crushed dried chillies (optional)

1 tsp ground cumin

pinch of sugar

4 eggs

salt

sprigs of fresh flat-leaf parsley to garnish

Preparation and cooking time: 30 minutes

Each serving provides Ⓥ

kcal 321, protein 19 g, fat 20 g (of which saturated fat 5 g), carbohydrate 18 g (of which sugars 17 g), fibre 6 g

✓✓✓	A, B₁₂, C, E, copper
✓✓	B₁, B₂, B₆, folate, niacin, iron, potassium, zinc
✓	calcium, selenium

1 Heat the oil in a deep, heavy-based frying pan. Add the onion, garlic, and red and green peppers, and cook gently for 5 minutes or until softened.

2 Stir in the tomatoes, tomato purée, chillies, if using, cumin, sugar, and salt to taste. Cover and cook gently for about 5 minutes or until the mixture is thick and well combined.

3 Make 4 hollows in the vegetable mixture using the back of a wooden spoon, then break an egg into each hollow. Cover the pan again and cook gently for 6–8 minutes or until the eggs are just set.

4 Serve immediately, straight from the pan, garnishing each plate with sprigs of parsley.

Some more ideas

• Add 55 g (2 oz) stoned black olives or chopped sun-dried tomatoes to the vegetable mixture.

• Instead of the chillies, add 1 tsp harissa sauce, or to taste.

• To make an omelette-like chakchouka, after breaking the eggs into the mixture, stir them gently to mix up the whites and yolks.

• For chakchouka with aubergine and mushrooms, replace the red and green peppers with 1 aubergine, cut into small chunks. In step 2, use 1 can chopped tomatoes, about 400 g, with the juice, instead of fresh tomatoes and add 170 g (6 oz) chopped button or chestnut mushrooms. Omit the chillies and cumin, and instead flavour with 1 tsp fennel or caraway seeds. Cover and cook gently for 15 minutes before breaking the eggs into the mixture.

Plus points

• Eggs are a useful source of vitamin A, but it is a myth that a darker-coloured yolk has a higher content of this vitamin (as carotene). The coloration is due to pigments found in grass and other food the chicken eats.

• Tomatoes are rich in the antioxidants vitamin C, beta-carotene and lycopene. Antioxidants help to protect the body's cells against the damaging effects of free radicals.

• The naturally waxy skin of peppers helps to protect against oxidation and thus against loss of vitamin C during storage. As a result, the vitamin C content remains high for several weeks after harvesting.

Sautéed tiger prawns with feta

In this quickly prepared supper dish, cubes of savoury feta cheese are briefly marinated in fresh ginger juice and soy sauce, then added to a crisp and colourful sauté of sugarsnap peas, mushrooms, spring onions and big tiger prawns. The sauté is served with rice cooked in vegetable stock to give it lots of flavour.

Serves 4

2.5 cm (1 in) piece fresh root ginger, coarsely grated

2 tsp light soy sauce

170 g (6 oz) feta cheese, cut into 2 cm (¾ in) cubes

1½ tbsp sunflower oil

225 g (8 oz) long-grain rice

750 ml (1¼ pints) vegetable stock

1 bunch spring onions, sliced on the diagonal

225 g (8 oz) small button mushrooms, halved

170 g (6 oz) sugarsnap peas, cut in half lengthways

12 large raw tiger prawns, peeled

2 tbsp chopped fresh coriander

1 tbsp chopped parsley

2 tbsp sesame seeds

salt and pepper

sprigs of fresh coriander to garnish

Preparation and cooking time: 30 minutes

Each serving provides

kcal 445, protein 21 g, fat 18 g (of which saturated fat 7 g), carbohydrate 53 g (of which sugars 3.5 g), fibre 3 g

✓✓✓	B_{12}, copper
✓✓	A, C, E, niacin, calcium, selenium, zinc
✓	B_1, B_2, B_6, folate, iron, potassium

1 Put the ginger in a garlic press and squeeze out the ginger juice into a small bowl. Mix in the soy sauce. Add the cubes of feta and gently toss to coat. Set aside to marinate while you cook the rice.

2 Heat ½ tbsp of the oil in a large saucepan, add the rice and fry gently for 2–3 minutes, stirring, until translucent. Slowly pour in the stock, still stirring, then cover the pan with a tight-fitting lid. Leave to cook over a low heat for 12–15 minutes or until the stock has been absorbed and the rice is tender.

3 Meanwhile, heat the remaining 1 tbsp oil in a sauté pan or large non-stick frying pan. Add the spring onions and mushrooms, and sauté for 1 minute, stirring. Add the sugarsnap peas and prawns, and sauté for a further 2–3 minutes, stirring frequently, until the prawns are pink and cooked through and all the vegetables are tender but still crisp.

4 Stir in the feta cheese with its marinade and cook gently for about 30 seconds, just to heat through, turning the cheese carefully to prevent it from breaking up too much. Sprinkle over the chopped coriander and parsley and the sesame seeds, and season with pepper to taste. Toss gently to mix.

5 Spoon the prawn and feta sauté onto warmed serving plates and garnish with sprigs of fresh coriander. Fluff up the rice with a fork, season with salt and pepper to taste, and serve with the stir-fry.

Plus points

• Feta cheese was traditionally made just from sheep's milk, but today goat's or cow's milk is often included. Feta has a lower fat content than many other cheeses, such as Cheddar, Edam and Parmesan.

• Like all seafish, prawns contain iodine. This essential mineral is required for proper functioning of the thyroid gland.

• Although sesame seeds are not used in any great amount in this recipe, they do provide some calcium, adding to that contributed by the feta cheese.

Some more ideas

● Instead of prawns, try 150 g (5½ oz) queen scallops or skinless salmon fillet, cut into 2 cm (¾ in) cubes. Use chopped fresh dill instead of coriander.

● For sautéed vegetables with Manchego cheese, drain 1 can of artichoke hearts in water, about 400 g; cut each artichoke into quarters and pat dry on kitchen paper. Heat 1 tbsp extra virgin olive oil in a large non-stick frying pan and sauté the artichokes until lightly browned. Remove and set aside. Add a further ½ tbsp extra virgin olive oil to the pan and sauté 170 g (6 oz) sliced baby leeks over a moderate heat for 1 minute. Add 1 large, seeded and sliced red pepper and 170 g (6 oz) thawed frozen broad beans. Cook for a further 3–4 minutes or until just tender. Return the artichoke quarters to the pan, together with 150 g (5½ oz) Manchego cheese, cut into 1 cm (½ in) cubes, 55 g (2 oz) pumpkin seeds, and salt and pepper to taste. Cook for a further 1–2 minutes, stirring gently, until all the vegetables are tender and the cheese is starting to melt. Serve hot, with the rice in the main recipe or with 8 large flour tortillas, warmed according to the packet instructions.

Eggs florentine

The term 'florentine' in a recipe title indicates that the dish uses spinach – in this case, poached eggs on a bed of spinach and leeks, coated with a cheese sauce. This updated version of the classic eggs florentine uses a lighter sauce thickened with cornflour rather than a butter and flour roux. Serve for supper with wholemeal toast.

Serves 4

20 g (¾ oz) cornflour

300 ml (10 fl oz) semi-skimmed milk

45 g (1½ oz) Gruyère cheese, finely grated

pinch of grated nutmeg

15 g (½ oz) butter

1 tbsp extra virgin olive oil

200 g (7 oz) baby leeks, thinly sliced

800 g (1¾ lb) baby spinach leaves

1 tsp vinegar

8 eggs

salt and pepper

paprika to garnish

Preparation and cooking time: 30 minutes

Each serving provides　　　Ⓥ

kcal 386, **protein** 27 g, **fat** 26 g (of which saturated fat 9 g), **carbohydrate** 13 g (of which sugars 8 g), **fibre** 5 g

✓✓✓	A, B₁₂, C, E, folate, calcium
✓✓	B₁, B₂, B₆, niacin, iron, potassium, selenium, zinc
✓	copper

1. First make the sauce. Mix the cornflour to a smooth paste with a little of the milk. Pour the remaining milk into a non-stick saucepan and bring to the boil. Stir the boiling milk into the cornflour mixture, then pour back into the saucepan. Bring to the boil, stirring. Once the sauce has thickened, simmer for 2 minutes. Remove from the heat, stir in the Gruyère, and season with nutmeg, salt and pepper to taste. Cover the surface of the sauce with a piece of greaseproof paper to prevent a skin from forming and set aside in a warm place.

2. Heat the butter with the olive oil in a large saucepan. Add the leeks and cook gently for about 3 minutes, stirring, until beginning to soften. Add the spinach and stir. Cover the pan and continue cooking over a moderate heat for 2–3 minutes or until the spinach has wilted and the leeks are tender. Drain the vegetables in a sieve, pressing down with the back of a spoon to remove excess moisture. Return to the pan and season with salt and pepper to taste. Cover to keep warm.

3. While the vegetables are cooking, poach the eggs. Half fill a large frying pan with water and bring to simmering point. Add the vinegar. Break in 4 of the eggs, one at a time, and cook gently for 3–4 minutes, spooning the hot water over the yolks towards the end of the cooking time. Lift out the eggs with a draining spoon and drain on kitchen paper. Poach the remaining eggs in the same way.

4. Preheat the grill to high. Spread the leek and spinach mixture in an even layer in a large flameproof dish. Make 8 hollows in the vegetables using the back of a spoon and place a poached egg in each hollow.

5. Spoon the cheese sauce over the eggs. Lightly dust with paprika, then place the dish under the grill. Cook for 3–4 minutes or until the top is lightly browned. Serve at once.

Plus points

- Like other animal foods, eggs provide useful amounts of vitamin B₁₂. Free-range eggs tend to contain more than eggs from battery hens.
- Spinach is a good source of nutrients with antioxidant properties, including vitamins C and E and carotenoid compounds.
- Leeks belong to the onion family. They provide vitamin E, and the green part of the leek is a good source of beta-carotene.

Another idea

● For bubble and squeak eggs, cook 400 g (14 oz) scrubbed and diced new potatoes in a large pan of boiling water for 7 minutes. Add 500 g (1 lb 2 oz) shredded spring greens to the pan and continue cooking for 4–5 minutes or until the vegetables are tender. Drain well, then return to the pan and crush together using a potato masher. Add 115 g (4 oz) diced cooked beetroot and carefully fold in. Season with salt and pepper to taste. Heat 1 tbsp extra virgin olive oil in a large non-stick frying pan with a flameproof handle. Transfer the vegetable mixture to the pan and spread it out evenly, pressing down with the back of a large spoon. Make 8 hollows in the vegetable mixture, then break an egg into each. Grate 55 g (2 oz) Lancashire cheese over the top, being sure to cover the whole surface. Cook under a preheated hot grill for 7–8 minutes or until the eggs are set. Serve hot, with French bread.

Venison Stroganoff

For a special main dish that takes only minutes to make, why not try this combination of tender strips of lean venison sautéed with fresh vegetables and finished with a soured cream sauce. With tagliatelle served alongside, plus a seasonal green vegetable such as broccoli florets, it makes a well-balanced meal.

Serves 4

2 tbsp sunflower oil

1 large onion, thinly sliced

1 yellow pepper, seeded and diced

300 g (10½ oz) tagliatelle

300 g (10½ oz) lean boneless venison, cut into thin strips

225 g (8 oz) button mushrooms, quartered

4 tbsp red wine

2 tbsp brandy

150 ml (5 fl oz) soured cream

5 tbsp chopped fresh flat-leaf parsley

2 tsp paprika

salt and pepper

Preparation time: 10 minutes
Cooking time: 20 minutes

Each serving provides

kcal 536, protein 29 g, fat 16 g (of which saturated fat 6 g), carbohydrate 66 g (of which sugars 9 g), fibre 5 g

✓✓✓	C, copper, zinc
✓✓	A, E, niacin, iron, potassium, selenium
✓	B$_1$, B$_2$, B$_6$, folate, calcium

1 Heat the oil in a large frying pan, add the onion and yellow pepper, and cook gently for 6–8 minutes or until softened.

2 Meanwhile, cook the tagliatelle in a large pan of boiling water for 10–12 minutes, or according to the packet instructions, until al dente.

3 Using a draining spoon, remove the onion and pepper from the frying pan and set aside. Add the venison strips and mushrooms to the pan, and sauté over a high heat for 3–4 minutes, stirring frequently, until the venison is just cooked.

4 Return the onion and pepper to the pan, and stir in the wine and brandy. Bring to the boil, then bubble for 3–4 minutes to reduce the liquid slightly, stirring frequently. Stir in the soured cream, 3 tbsp of the parsley, the paprika, and salt and pepper to taste. Heat through gently.

5 Drain the pasta well and divide among 4 warmed plates. Spoon the venison Stroganoff onto the plates and garnish with the remaining 2 tbsp parsley. Serve hot.

Some more ideas

• Instead of venison, you can use lean rump or fillet steak, pork fillet (tenderloin) or skinless boneless chicken breasts (fillets).

• For a flageolet and vegetable Stroganoff, sauté 2 sliced leeks, 1 seeded and sliced red or green pepper, 2 sliced courgettes (or 1 diced small aubergine) and 115 g (4 oz) sliced mushrooms in 2 tbsp sunflower oil for about 15 minutes or until tender. Add 1 can flageolet beans, about 410 g, drained and rinsed, 2 tbsp chopped fresh mixed herbs (or 2 tsp dried herbes de Provence) and 6 tbsp dry white wine or vegetable stock. Bring to the boil and simmer for 3–4 minutes or until the vegetable mixture is piping hot. Stir in 150 ml (5 fl oz) soured cream, and salt and pepper to taste. Serve with 250 g (8½ oz) mixed basmati and wild rice, steamed for 15 minutes, or cooked according to the packet instructions, until tender.

Plus points

• Soured cream has a much lower fat content than most other creams, yet still adds a rich, creamy texture to a sauce.

• Venison is an excellent source of protein. Because it is very lean, it is lower in fat than other red meats.

• Parsley is an excellent source of vitamin C – just 1 tsp of chopped parsley can make a significant contribution to the recommended daily requirement.

Stuffed Thai omelette

For these delectable chilli-flavoured omelettes, the eggs are whisked with cornflour to give them a slightly firmer texture, suitable for folding round a colourful filling of stir-fried vegetables and rice noodles.

Serves 4

4 tsp cornflour

8 eggs

¼–½ tsp crushed dried chillies, to taste

2 tbsp sunflower oil

125 g (4½ oz) fine rice noodles

1 tsp toasted sesame oil

115 g (4 oz) chestnut mushrooms, sliced

2 carrots, cut into 5 cm (2 in) matchstick strips

1 small green pepper, seeded and cut into thin strips

170 g (6 oz) white cabbage, finely shredded

2 tbsp light soy sauce

2 tsp white wine vinegar

2 tsp chopped root ginger bottled in oil

salt and pepper

1 tbsp toasted sesame seeds to garnish (optional)

Preparation and cooking time: 30 minutes

Each serving provides

kcal 401, **protein** 18.5 g, **fat** 20 g (of which saturated fat 4 g), **carbohydrate** 38 g (of which sugars 7 g), **fibre** 3 g

✓✓✓	A, B₁₂, C
✓✓	B₂, E, folate, niacin, copper, selenium, zinc
✓	B₁, B₆, calcium, iron, potassium

1 Mix the cornflour with 3 tbsp cold water in a mixing bowl. Add the eggs and whisk together until mixed. Stir in the chillies and season with salt and pepper to taste.

2 Heat 1 tsp of the sunflower oil in a 20 cm (8 in) non-stick frying pan over a moderate heat. Pour in one-quarter of the egg mixture, tipping the pan to spread out the egg in a thin, even layer. Cook for 2 minutes or until set and golden brown underneath.

3 Slide the omelette out of the pan onto a plate. Make 3 more omelettes in the same way, stacking them up interleaved with greaseproof paper. Keep warm.

4 While making the omelettes, soak the rice noodles in boiling water to cover for 4 minutes, or according to the packet instructions, then drain.

5 Heat the remaining 2 tsp sunflower oil with the toasted sesame oil in a wok or large frying pan. Add the mushrooms, carrots, green pepper and cabbage, and stir-fry for 4–5 minutes or until just tender. Add the soy sauce, vinegar, ginger and softened rice noodles. Gently toss together until piping hot.

6 Divide the vegetable and noodle mixture among the omelettes and fold them over in half. Sprinkle with the sesame seeds and serve immediately.

Another idea

● For a folded salad omelette, grill 2 rashers of lean back bacon until crisp, then crumble or chop. Whisk the eggs with the cornflour and water as in the main recipe, but leave out the chillies. For each omelette, heat 1 tsp sunflower oil in a 20 cm (8 in) non-stick frying pan, sprinkle one-quarter of the bacon pieces evenly over the bottom of the pan and then pour in one-quarter of the egg mixture. Cook the omelettes as in the main recipe, then slide onto serving plates and leave to cool. Finely shred ½ small iceberg lettuce and mix with 2 chopped celery sticks, 1 seeded and thinly sliced red pepper and 6 chopped spring onions. Season to taste. Spread half of each omelette with 2 tbsp hummus and top with the salad mixture. Fold the omelettes over in half and serve.

Plus points

● Rice noodles contain no gluten and are therefore suitable for people with coeliac disease who are unable to tolerate gluten-containing food.

● White cabbage contains beneficial phytochemicals including glucosinolates, which have strong anti-cancer effects.

Chickpea and vegetable eggah

Popular throughout the Middle East, this thick and chunky Arab omelette is served flat, not rolled or folded, and is more like a cake. It is packed with vegetables and chickpeas, and is equally delicious hot or cold – ideal for a picnic. Serve with a simple tomato and red onion salad, and flat Arab bread.

quick egg and dairy dishes

Serves 4

3 tbsp extra virgin olive oil

1 small onion, chopped

1 garlic clove, crushed

1 tsp ground cumin

1 tsp ground coriander

pinch of cayenne pepper

250 g (8½ oz) new potatoes, scrubbed and cut into 1 cm (½ in) dice

1 small red pepper, seeded and diced

1 small aubergine, about 200 g (7 oz), cut into 1 cm (½ in) dice

1 can chickpeas, about 410 g, drained and rinsed

6 eggs

2 tbsp chopped fresh coriander

salt and pepper

Preparation and cooking time: 30 minutes

Each serving provides Ⓥ

kcal 341, **protein** 18 g, **fat** 20 g (of which saturated fat 4 g), **carbohydrate** 24 g (of which sugars 5 g), **fibre** 5 g

✓✓✓	A, B₁₂, C
✓✓	zinc
✓	B₁, B₂, B₆, E, folate, niacin, calcium, copper, iron, potassium, selenium

1 Heat 1 tbsp of the oil in a 25 cm (10 in) non-stick frying pan with a flameproof handle. Add the onion and cook for 2–3 minutes or until starting to soften. Stir in the garlic, cumin, ground coriander and cayenne pepper, and continue cooking for 1 minute, stirring constantly.

2 Add a further 1 tbsp of the oil to the frying pan, then add the potatoes, red pepper and aubergine. Continue frying for 5 minutes, stirring frequently, until the vegetables are lightly browned.

3 Add 5 tbsp water, cover and steam for 5 minutes. Then remove the lid and continue cooking until all excess liquid has evaporated. Stir in the chickpeas.

4 Lightly beat the eggs in a large mixing bowl. Add the chopped coriander and season with salt and pepper to taste. Tip in the vegetable and chickpea mixture from the pan and stir to mix.

5 Preheat the grill to high. Heat the remaining 1 tbsp oil in the frying pan over a moderate heat. Pour in the egg mixture, spreading the vegetables out evenly. Cook the eggah, shaking the pan from time to time, for 3–4 minutes or until almost set – there will still be some uncooked egg mixture on the top.

6 Place the pan under the grill and cook the eggah for about 2 minutes or until the top looks set. Remove from the heat and allow the eggah to rest in the pan for 2 minutes, then slide it onto a serving plate or board. Serve hot, cut into wedges.

Another idea

• For a salmon and butter bean eggah, omit the cumin, ground coriander and aubergine, and add 2 diced courgettes with the water in step 3. Replace the chickpeas with 1 can butter beans, about 410 g, drained and rinsed. In step 4, add 1 can salmon, about 200 g, drained and flaked, 2 tbsp chopped fresh dill, 1 tbsp snipped fresh chives and the finely grated zest of 1 lemon to the beaten eggs with the vegetables and beans.

Plus points

• New potatoes cooked in their skins have a higher fibre content than peeled potatoes. The nutrients just under the skin are also preserved when potatoes are only scrubbed and not peeled.

• Chickpeas, like other pulses, are a good source of dietary fibre, particularly the insoluble type that can help to lower high levels of blood cholesterol.

Satisfying Main Dishes

For family meals or for entertaining

Basing meals on protein-rich eggs, milk and cheese makes good nutritional sense. And because these foods are so versatile, there is a wide variety of exciting dishes that can be created. Use them in a cheesy choux pastry ring called a gougère and fill the centre with a roasted ratatouille, or roll lacy pancakes round Camembert and broccoli and bake in a tomato sauce. Make the easy Indian cheese called paneer and add it to a fragrant green pea curry. Or try a classic French batter pudding flavoured with pecorino and studded with cherry tomatoes.

Cheshire and root vegetable gratin

This country-style gratin tops nutty-flavoured root vegetables with a crisp mixture of wholemeal bread cubes and Cheshire cheese. It makes a really satisfying main dish on a chilly day. Serve in the baking dish, straight from the oven, with a leafy green vegetable or mixed salad alongside.

Serves 4

200 g (7 oz) carrots, thinly sliced.

250 g (8½ oz) parsnips, thinly sliced

300 g (10½ oz) celeriac, thinly sliced

400 g (14 oz) potatoes, peeled and thinly sliced

3 tbsp chopped fresh chives

½ tsp freshly grated nutmeg

200 ml (7 fl oz) semi-skimmed milk

75 g (2½ oz) fromage frais

4 tbsp soured cream

2 thick slices wholemeal bread, about 85 g (3 oz) in total

15 g (½ oz) butter, melted

100 g (3½ oz) Cheshire cheese, finely grated

salt and pepper

Preparation and cooking time: 1¾–2 hours

1 Preheat the oven to 180°C (350°F, gas mark 4). Layer the carrot, parsnip, celeriac and potato slices in a large, shallow ovenproof dish, sprinkling the chives, nutmeg, and salt and pepper to taste between the layers.

2 In a mixing bowl, lightly whisk together the milk, fromage frais and soured cream, then pour evenly over the vegetables. Cover the dish with foil and bake for 1–1¼ hours or until the vegetables are tender.

3 Cut the bread into 5 mm (¼ in) dice and toss with the melted butter and grated cheese to mix evenly. Spoon the mixture in an even layer over the vegetables. Return to the oven, without the foil covering, and bake for a further 15–20 minutes or until the top is crisp and golden. Serve hot.

Some more ideas

• For a slightly stronger onion flavour, replace the chives with a bunch of spring onions, chopped, or 1 thinly sliced leek.

• Other British cheeses can be used in place of Cheshire, such as Wensleydale or Lancashire. Or use Emmenthal cheese.

• To make a Cheddar and sweet potato gratin, peel and thinly slice 600 g (1 lb 5 oz) sweet potatoes and layer in a large, shallow ovenproof dish with 200 g (7 oz) thinly sliced celery and 1 thinly sliced onion, sprinkling the layers with 1 tbsp chopped fresh thyme, 1 tsp caraway seeds, and salt and pepper to taste. Instead of soured cream, whisk 4 tbsp single cream with the fromage frais and milk. For the topping, mix 85 g (3 oz) fresh wholemeal breadcrumbs with 15 g (½ oz) melted butter and 100 g (3½ oz) grated Cheddar cheese.

Plus points

• Cheshire cheese is believed to be one of the oldest of all English cheeses. It is available white or orangey-red (coloured with a vegetable dye). Nutritionally there is no difference between the 2 varieties.

• Root vegetables are inexpensive and a good source of carbohydrate and fibre.

• Carrots are an important source of beta-carotene, the precursor of vitamin A.

Each serving provides Ⓥ

kcal 400, **protein** 16 g, **fat** 19 g (of which saturated fat 11 g), **carbohydrate** 44 g (of which sugars 14 g), **fibre** 9 g

✓✓✓	A
✓✓	B₁, B₆, C, folate, calcium, potassium, zinc
✓	B₂, B₁₂, E, niacin, copper, iron, selenium

Baked aubergines with yogurt

In this delicious supper dish, grilled slices of aubergine and courgette are layered with a rich tomato sauce and cumin-flavoured yogurt, then baked. Thick slices of Greek daktyla bread – topped with sesame, black onion and anise seeds – and a crisp green salad are perfect accompaniments.

Serves 4

3 tbsp extra virgin olive oil

1 red onion, finely chopped

2 garlic cloves, finely chopped

1 can chopped tomatoes, about 400 g

2 tsp sun-dried tomato paste

6 tbsp dry red wine

1 bay leaf

2 tbsp chopped parsley

3 aubergines, about 675 g (1½ lb) in total, cut into 1 cm (½ in) slices

3 courgettes, about 450 g (1 lb) in total, thinly sliced

½ tsp ground cumin

400 g (14 oz) plain low-fat yogurt

2 eggs, beaten

30 g (1 oz) Parmesan cheese, freshly grated

salt and pepper

Preparation time: about 50 minutes

Cooking time: 40–45 minutes

Each serving provides   Ⓥ

kcal 304, **protein** 17 g, **fat** 16 g (of which saturated fat 4 g), **carbohydrate** 20 g (of which sugars 18.5 g), **fibre** 6 g

✓✓✓	C, calcium
✓✓	A, B₆, B₁₂, folate, copper, potassium, zinc
✓	B₁, B₂, E, niacin, iron, selenium

1 Heat 1 tbsp of the oil in a saucepan, add the onion and cook for about 8 minutes or until softened. Add the garlic and cook for a further minute, stirring. Stir in the chopped tomatoes with their juice, the tomato paste, wine and bay leaf. Cover and simmer gently for 10 minutes.

2 Uncover the pan and let the sauce bubble for a further 10 minutes or until thickened, stirring occasionally. Remove the bay leaf. Stir in the parsley and season with salt and pepper to taste.

3 While the sauce is simmering, preheat the grill to moderate. Lightly brush the aubergine and courgette slices with the remaining 2 tbsp oil. Cook under the grill, in batches, for 3–4 minutes on each side or until browned and very tender.

4 Preheat the oven to 180°C (350°F, gas mark 4). Stir the cumin into half of the yogurt.

5 Arrange one-third of the aubergine slices, in one layer, in a large ovenproof dish that is about 2.5 litres (4 pints) capacity. Spoon over half of the tomato sauce. Arrange half of the courgette slices on top, in one layer, then drizzle with half of the cumin-flavoured yogurt. Repeat the layers, then finish with a layer of the remaining aubergine slices.

6 Mix the remaining 200 g (7 oz) yogurt with the beaten eggs and half of the Parmesan. Spoon the yogurt mixture over the aubergines, spreading with the back of the spoon to cover evenly. Sprinkle with the remaining Parmesan.

7 Bake for 40–45 minutes or until the top is lightly browned and set, and the sauce is bubbling. Serve hot, in the baking dish.

Plus points

- The normal gut flora can be upset by antibiotics, stress and poor diet. Including yogurt in the diet helps to maintain the 'good' bacteria in the gut and prevent the growth of less desirable bacteria.

- Aubergines are a useful vegetable to include in dishes, because they add bulk and dietary fibre without adding calories – 100 g (3½ oz) contains just 15 kcal.

- Flavonoids are compounds found in onions, which can help to protect against heart disease. Although they occur in both red and white onions, red onions have been shown to have higher levels of flavonoids.

Another idea

● For a chicken, spinach and yogurt layered bake, cook 2 large sliced leeks in lightly boiling water for 4–5 minutes or until just tender. Drain and spread half over the bottom of a large ovenproof dish that is 1.7 litres (3 pints) capacity. Cut 300 g (10½ oz) cooked skinless boneless chicken breasts (fillets) into thick slices and arrange on top of the leeks. Set aside. Pack 450 g (1 lb) rinsed spinach into a large saucepan, cover and cook gently for 2–3 minutes, shaking the pan occasionally, until the spinach is wilted. Drain in a colander, but do not squeeze dry. Soften 2 finely chopped shallots in 15 g (½ oz) butter in the wiped-out saucepan. Add 1 crushed garlic clove and cook for a further minute. Stir in 170 g (6 oz) curd cheese, 3 tbsp semi-skimmed milk, 1 tsp wholegrain mustard, a pinch of freshly grated nutmeg, and salt and pepper to taste. Heat gently, stirring, until smoothly blended, then stir in the spinach. Spoon the mixture over the chicken and spread the remaining leeks on top. Mix 150 g (5½ oz) plain low-fat yogurt with 15 g (½ oz) grated Gruyère cheese, 1 beaten egg, and seasoning to taste. Spoon over the leeks and sprinkle with a further 15 g (½ oz) grated Gruyère. Bake in a preheated 180ºC (350ºF, gas mark 4) oven for 35 minutes. Leave to stand for 5 minutes, then serve with jacket baked potatoes.

Tomato and pecorino clafoutis

For this savoury version of a classic French batter pudding, sweet cherry tomatoes are baked in a light, fluffy batter flavoured with grated pecorino cheese. Make individual clafoutis, or one large one, and serve for a simple lunch or supper with crusty bread or boiled new potatoes and green beans.

Serves 4

2 tsp extra virgin olive oil

450 g (1 lb) cherry tomatoes

4 tbsp snipped fresh chives

85 g (3 oz) mature pecorino cheese, coarsely grated

6 large eggs

45 g (1½ oz) plain flour

3 tbsp soured cream

300 ml (10 fl oz) semi-skimmed milk

Preparation time: 20 minutes
Cooking time: 30–35 minutes

1 Preheat the oven to 190°C (375°F, gas mark 5). Lightly oil 4 shallow ovenproof dishes, each 12–15 cm (5–6 in) in diameter. Divide the cherry tomatoes among the dishes, spreading them out, and sprinkle over the chives and 75 g (2½ oz) of the cheese.

2 Break the eggs into a bowl and whisk them together, then gradually whisk in the flour until smooth. Add the soured cream, then gradually whisk in the milk to make a thin, smooth batter. Season with salt and pepper to taste.

3 Pour the batter over the tomatoes, dividing it evenly among the dishes. Sprinkle over the remaining cheese and an extra grinding of pepper. Bake for 30–35 minutes or until set, puffed and lightly golden.

4 Remove the clafoutis from the oven and leave to cool for a few minutes before serving, as the tomatoes are very hot inside.

Some more ideas

● Bake one large clafoutis, using a lightly oiled 23 cm (9 in) round ovenproof dish that is about 5 cm (2 in) deep. Increase the baking time to 35–40 minutes.

● Use torn fresh basil leaves or chopped fresh oregano instead of chives.

● For a Red Leicester and onion clafoutis, cut 250 g (8½ oz) red onions into thin wedges and fry in 1 tbsp extra virgin olive oil for about 5 minutes or until golden. Stir in 1 tbsp fresh thyme leaves towards the end of the cooking. Scatter the onions over the bottom of a lightly oiled 23 cm (9 in) round ovenproof dish that is about 5 cm (2 in) deep. Coarsely grate 85 g (3 oz) red Leicester cheese and sprinkle all but a small handful of it over the onions. Make the batter as in the main recipe and pour over the onions. Give the mixture a stir, then sprinkle over the remaining cheese and a few sprigs of fresh thyme. Bake for 35–40 minutes or until puffed and golden.

Plus points

● Pecorino is a hard Italian cheese made from sheep's milk. Like Parmesan, it is quite high in fat, but need only be used in small quantities as it has a rich, strong flavour.

● Both soured cream and single cream – the fresh version of soured cream – contain considerably more calcium than other creams.

● Tomatoes contain lycopene, a valuable antioxidant that may help to protect against prostate, bladder and pancreatic cancers if tomatoes are included in the diet regularly.

Each serving provides

kcal 392, protein 26 g, fat 26 g (of which saturated fat 11 g), carbohydrate 17 g (of which sugars 8 g), fibre 1.5 g

✓✓✓	B₁₂, calcium
✓✓	A, B₂, C, E, niacin, zinc
✓	B₁, B₆, folate, copper, iron, potassium, selenium

satisfying main dishes

Roasted vegetable and pasta bake

A hearty vegetarian dish packed with flavour, this is ideal for a family meal or casual entertaining. A selection of vegetables – butternut squash, asparagus and leeks – is roasted in garlicky olive oil, then tossed with chunky pasta shapes and a cheesy sauce. The final baking is done in the roasting tin, which saves on washing up.

Serves 4

1 small butternut squash, peeled, seeded and cut into 5 cm (2 in) cubes, about 450 g (1 lb) peeled weight

2 red onions, cut into large chunks

2 garlic cloves, thinly sliced

2 tbsp extra virgin olive oil

500 g (1 lb 2 oz) leeks, thickly sliced

170 g (6 oz) asparagus spears, cut across in half

300 g (10½ oz) rigatoni or penne

600 ml (1 pint) semi-skimmed milk

3 tbsp cornflour

75 g (2½ oz) extra mature Cheddar cheese, grated

2 tsp wholegrain mustard

salt and pepper

Preparation and cooking time: about 1¼ hours

Each serving provides Ⓥ

kcal 619, **protein** 24 g, **fat** 17 g (of which saturated fat 7 g), **carbohydrate** 98 g (of which sugars 22 g), **fibre** 9 g

✓✓✓	A, B₁, C, folate, calcium
✓✓	B₆, B₁₂, E, niacin, copper, iron, potassium, selenium, zinc
✓	B₂

1 Preheat the oven to 220°C (425°F, gas mark 7). Put the squash and red onions in a large roasting tin and scatter over the sliced garlic. Drizzle with the oil and season with salt and pepper to taste. Toss to coat the vegetables with the oil, then place the tin in the oven and roast for 15 minutes.

2 Remove the tin from the oven and add the leeks and asparagus. Toss gently to mix with the other vegetables, then return to the oven. Roast for a further 20 minutes or until all the vegetables are tender and beginning to brown.

3 Meanwhile, cook the pasta in a large saucepan of boiling water for 10–12 minutes, or according to the packet instructions, until al dente.

4 While the pasta is cooking, make the sauce. Measure 4 tbsp of the cold milk into a jug, add the cornflour and stir to make a smooth paste. Heat the remaining milk in a saucepan until almost boiling. Stir the hot milk into the cornflour mixture, then return to the saucepan and heat gently, stirring, until the mixture boils and thickens. Simmer for 2 minutes.

5 Remove the sauce from the heat and add about two-thirds of the cheese and the mustard. Season with salt and pepper to taste.

6 Take the tin of roasted vegetables from the oven. Drain the pasta well in a colander, then tip on top of the vegetables and stir to combine. Stir in the sauce. Sprinkle the remaining cheese evenly over the top. Return to the oven and bake for 10–15 minutes or until golden and bubbling. Serve hot.

Plus points

● The bright orange flesh of butternut squash is an indicator of its high beta-carotene content. Squash is also a good source of vitamin C and a useful source of vitamin E.

● Milk is one of the best sources of calcium in the diet. Calcium is a vital mineral needed to ensure strong, healthy bones and teeth, and for the proper functioning of muscles and nerves.

● Asparagus contains a phytochemical called asparagine, which has a strong diuretic effect. Herbalists recommend eating asparagus as a treatment for rheumatism and the bloating associated with PMT.

Another idea

● To make roasted vegetable lasagne, combine the red onions and asparagus in a roasting tin and add 2 seeded and sliced red peppers and 3 thickly sliced courgettes. Toss with the garlic, oil and seasoning, then roast for 25 minutes. Remove from the oven, and lower it to 190ºC (375ºF, gas mark 5). Stir 2 cans of chopped tomatoes, about 400 g each, with their juices, into the vegetable mixture. In a rectangular ovenproof dish, measuring about 23 x 30 cm (9 x 12 in), layer the vegetable mixture with 200 g (7 oz) no-precook lasagne sheets, 150 g (5½ oz) roughly chopped feta cheese and 15 g (½ oz) shredded fresh basil, starting with a layer of vegetables and ending with a layer of lasagne. Season 300 ml (10 fl oz) fromage frais to taste, and stir in 25 g (scant 1 oz) freshly grated Parmesan cheese. Spread evenly over the top of the lasagne. Bake for 30–35 minutes or until golden. Serve hot.

Cheese and onion bread pudding

A simple, homely dish of diced challah bread baked in a cheesy custard with leeks and spring onions makes great comfort food, and is an excellent way to use up slightly stale bread. Serve with a crisp salad of cos or Little Gem lettuce leaves tossed with sliced cucumber and halved cherry tomatoes.

Serves 4

340 g (12 oz) day-old challah bread
600 ml (1 pint) semi-skimmed milk
3 eggs
pinch of crushed dried chillies
100 g (3½ oz) Emmenthal cheese, grated
2 leeks, thinly sliced
4 spring onions, thinly sliced
2 tbsp freshly grated Parmesan cheese
salt and pepper

Preparation time: 20 minutes
Cooking time: 30 minutes

Each serving provides Ⓥ

kcal 469, protein 28 g, fat 18 g (of which saturated fat 9 g), carbohydrate 52 g (of which sugars 11 g), fibre 3 g

✓✓✓	A, B$_{12}$, calcium, copper, selenium
✓✓	B$_1$, B$_2$, B$_6$, C, folate, niacin, zinc
✓	E, iron, potassium

1 Cut the bread into small cubes about 1 cm (½ in) square. Put the bread into a large mixing bowl, pour over the milk and leave to soak for 15 minutes.

2 Meanwhile, preheat the oven to 180°C (350°F, gas mark 4). Break the eggs into a small mixing bowl and add the chillies, and salt and pepper to taste. Beat lightly together with a fork. Add the Emmenthal cheese, leeks and spring onions, and stir to combine.

3 Add the egg mixture to the soaked bread cubes. Fold together gently but thoroughly, then pour into a lightly greased 2 litre (3½ pint) shallow ovenproof dish.

4 Sprinkle the grated Parmesan evenly over the surface, then bake for 30 minutes or until puffed and just set, and the top is crisp and golden. Serve hot.

Some more ideas

• Make sun-dried tomato bread pudding with peppers. Thickly slice 340 g (12 oz) day-old sun-dried tomato-flavoured bread. Cut 100 g (3½ oz) Emmenthal cheese into thin slices and use to make sandwiches with the bread. Cut the sandwiches in half, then arrange in a single layer in a lightly greased 2 litre (3½ pint) shallow ovenproof dish. Scatter over 3 seeded and finely diced peppers (1 green, 1 yellow and 1 red). Beat 3 eggs with 600 ml (1 pint) semi-skimmed milk, 2 tbsp sun-dried tomato paste, and salt and pepper to taste. Pour over the sandwiches and leave to soak for 15 minutes. Sprinkle the surface with 2 tbsp freshly grated Parmesan cheese and bake as in the main recipe.

• For olive bread pudding, in the sun-dried tomato bread pudding above, use olive bread instead of sun-dried tomato bread and replace the sun-dried tomato paste with tapenade (black olive paste).

Plus points

• Emmenthal, a Swiss cheese made from cow's milk, has a sweet and nutty flavour. With the other dairy products used here, it makes a significant contribution to the total protein and calcium content of the dish.

• Challah bread, which is enriched with egg, is a good source of starchy carbohydrate. At least half the calories in a healthy diet should come from starchy foods.

• Both the white bulb and green leaves of spring onions are edible, and using the leaves increases the amount of carotene in this dish.

Provençal Swiss chard tian

In this colourful, vitamin-rich dish, rice and leafy Swiss chard are layered with sliced tomatoes and baked in a Gruyère-flavoured custard. The name of the dish –'tian'– comes from the earthenware casserole in which such mixtures of vegetables, rice and eggs are traditionally baked in Provence.

Serves 4

250 g (8½ oz) long-grain rice
400 g (14 oz) Swiss chard
100 g (3½ oz) Gruyère cheese, grated
1 tbsp chopped fresh thyme
340 g (12 oz) tomatoes, sliced
3 eggs, beaten
200 ml (7 fl oz) semi-skimmed milk
salt and pepper

Preparation time: 15 minutes
Cooking time: 45 minutes

Each serving provides ⓥ

kcal 451, **protein** 21 g, **fat** 15 g (of which saturated fat 7 g), **carbohydrate** 63 g (of which sugars 6 g), **fibre** 1 g

✓✓✓	A, B$_{12}$, C, folate, calcium
✓✓	niacin, zinc
✓	B$_1$, B$_2$, B$_6$, E, copper, iron, potassium, selenium

1 Preheat the oven to 180°C (350°F, gas mark 4). Cook the rice in boiling water for 10–15 minutes, or according to the packet instructions, until just tender. Drain well.

2 Trim the stalks from the chard and chop. Cut the chard leaves into 2 cm (¾ in) slices. Drop the stalks into a large pan of boiling water and cook for 2 minutes. Add the chard leaves and cook for a further 1–2 minutes. Drain well in a colander, then refresh under cold running water. Press out excess liquid.

3 Mix together the chard and rice, then stir in about half of the grated Gruyère, the thyme, and salt and pepper to taste.

4 Lightly grease a 2 litre (3½ pint) tian (earthenware casserole) or a shallow ovenproof dish. Spoon half the rice mixture into the dish, spreading evenly. Add a layer of half the tomato slices, then spoon over the remaining rice mixture.

5 Whisk together the eggs and milk in a measuring jug. Pour evenly over the rice mixture. Arrange the remaining tomato slices on top and sprinkle with the rest of the Gruyère. Bake for about 45 minutes or until lightly set and the top is beginning to brown. Serve hot.

Some more ideas

• Use spring greens instead of Swiss chard. There is no need to separate the stalks and leaves, and cooking time is 2–3 minutes.

• For a courgette and mushroom loaf, melt 25 g (scant 1 oz) butter in a frying pan and cook 350 g (12½ oz) sliced courgettes and 200 g (7 oz) sliced mushrooms with a crushed garlic clove until golden. Add to the cooked rice, together with the eggs, milk, 3 tbsp chopped parsley and 100 g (3½ oz) grated Cheddar cheese. Season to taste. Pour into a greased and bottom-lined 1.2 litre (2 pint) loaf tin and smooth the surface. Bake in a preheated 180°C (350°F, gas mark 4) oven for about 1 hour or until just set. Leave to cool for 5 minutes, then run a knife round the sides of the loaf and turn out. Serve with a chunky tomato sauce made by cooking canned chopped tomatoes until thick.

Plus points

• Leafy greens like Swiss chard are a good source of vitamins C, E, K and folate, as well as minerals such as calcium.

• Rice is a low-fat starchy carbohydrate, an ideal foodstuff to include in a healthy diet. It is also gluten-free and therefore suitable for those with coeliac disease.

satisfying main dishes

Pea curry with Indian paneer

Paneer is an Indian cheese, similar to ricotta but drier. It's often combined with peas in a curry. This delicious version uses home-made paneer, which is simple to make. Serve with basmati rice for a well-balanced meal.

Serves 4

Paneer

2.3 litres (4 pints) full-fat milk

6 tbsp lemon juice

Pea and tomato curry

3 tbsp sunflower oil

1 large onion, chopped

2 garlic cloves, finely chopped

5 cm (2 in) piece fresh root ginger, finely chopped

1 fresh green chilli, seeded and thinly sliced

1 tbsp coriander seeds, crushed

1 tbsp cumin seeds, crushed

1 tsp turmeric

1 tbsp garam masala

450 g (1 lb) firm tomatoes, quartered

340 g (12 oz) frozen peas

85 g (3 oz) spinach leaves

15 g (½ oz) fresh coriander, roughly chopped

salt

Preparation time: 15 minutes, plus about 45 minutes draining and 3 hours pressing

Cooking time: about 20 minutes

Each serving provides Ⓥ

kcal 298, **protein** 20 g, **fat** 15 g (of which saturated fat 5 g), **carbohydrate** 22 g (of which sugars 14 g), **fibre** 7 g

✓✓✓	A, C, E
✓✓	B₁, B₁₂, folate, niacin, calcium, zinc
✓	B₂, B₆, copper, iron, potassium

1 First make the paneer. Pour the milk into a large saucepan and bring to the boil. Immediately reduce the heat to low and add the lemon juice. Stir for 1–2 minutes or until the milk separates into curds and whey. Remove the pan from the heat.

2 Line a large sieve or colander with muslin, or a clean, tight-knit dishcloth, and set over a large bowl. Pour in the milk mixture. Leave to drain for about 15 minutes or until cool.

3 Bring together the corners of the muslin or cloth to make a bundle containing the drained curds. Squeeze them, then leave to drain for a further 30 minutes or until all the whey has dripped though the sieve into the bowl. Reserve 240 ml (8 fl oz) of the whey.

4 Keeping the curds wrapped in the muslin or cloth, place on a board. Set another board on top and press down to flatten the ball shape into an oblong block. Place cans or weights on top and leave in a cool place for about 3 hours or until firm.

5 Carefully peel off the muslin and cut the cheese into squares about 2 cm (¾ in). Heat 1 tbsp of the oil in a large non-stick frying pan and cook the paneer for 1–2 minutes on each side or until golden. As the pieces are browned, remove from the pan with a draining spoon and set aside.

6 For the curry, heat the remaining 2 tbsp oil in the pan. Add the onion and cook gently for 5 minutes or until softened. Stir in the garlic and ginger, and cook gently for 1 minute, then stir in the chilli, coriander and cumin seeds, turmeric and garam masala. Cook for 1 more minute, stirring constantly.

7 Add the tomatoes, the reserved whey and a pinch of salt, and stir well to mix. Cover and cook gently for 5 minutes.

8 Add the peas and bring back to the boil, then reduce the heat, cover again and simmer for 5 minutes. Add the spinach, stirring it in gently so as not to break up the tomatoes too much. Simmer for 3–4 minutes or until the spinach has just wilted and the peas are hot and tender.

9 Stir in most of the chopped fresh coriander, then transfer the curry to a serving dish and scatter the paneer on top. Spoon the curry gently over the paneer to warm it, then sprinkle with the rest of the coriander and serve.

Plus point

• This home-made paneer is low in fat and very nutritious, providing protein, calcium and vitamins, including vitamins A and D.

Some more ideas

● Use frozen minted peas.

● For a cottage cheese and vegetable curry, which is similar but much quicker to make, cook 600 g (1 lb 5 oz) peeled potatoes, cut into large chunks, in a large pan of boiling water for 5 minutes. Add 400 g (14 oz) cauliflower florets to the pan and cook for 5 more minutes. Finally, add 200 g (7 oz) halved fine green beans and cook for a further 3–4 minutes or until all the vegetables are tender. While the vegetables are cooking, place 350 g (12½ oz) cottage cheese in a sieve and leave to drain off any excess liquid. Cook the onion and spices as in step 6 of the main recipe, then add 300 ml (10 fl oz) vegetable stock and cook gently for a further 5 minutes. Add the drained potatoes, cauliflower and beans to the spiced sauce and stir to coat. Season with salt to taste. Fold in the cottage cheese and heat through gently. Serve hot, with wholewheat parathas or naan bread.

Pumpkin, ricotta and sage gnocchi

There are numerous versions of gnocchi in Italy. For the one here, a flour-based dough of ricotta and mashed pumpkin, flavoured with sage and Parmesan cheese, is shaped into the little dumplings. A colourful roasted pepper and onion sauce completes the dish. Serve with a baby spinach and watercress salad.

Serves 4

2 red peppers, halved and seeded

1 onion, halved

500 g (1 lb 2 oz) pumpkin or acorn squash, cut into wedges and seeded

1 tbsp extra virgin olive oil

250 g (8½ oz) ricotta cheese

1 egg, beaten

3 tbsp chopped fresh sage

30 g (1 oz) Parmesan cheese, freshly grated

200 g (7 oz) plain flour, plus extra for rolling

salt and pepper

fresh sage leaves to garnish

Preparation and cooking time: 1½–2 hours, plus 1–2 hours drying

1 Preheat the oven to 200ºC (400ºF, gas mark 6). Spread out the pepper and onion halves, cut side down, on a baking sheet. Place the pumpkin or squash wedges, skin side up, on another baking sheet. Bake the peppers and onion for 30–35 minutes, and the pumpkin or squash for 45–55 minutes, or until all the vegetables are tender.

2 Transfer the peppers and onions to a blender or food processor and add the oil. Blend until almost smooth. Season with salt and pepper to taste. Pour into a saucepan and set aside.

3 Leave the pumpkin or squash until cool enough to handle, then scrape the flesh from the skins into a bowl. Mash until smooth. Beat in the ricotta, egg, chopped sage and Parmesan, then gradually work in the flour to make a soft dough.

4 Flour a work surface. Divide the dough into quarters and, with floured hands, roll each piece into a long, 2 cm (¾ in) thick rope. Cut into 2 cm (¾ in) lengths. Press the back of a fork into each piece of dough to make a pattern. Leave the gnocchi at room temperature to dry for 1–2 hours.

5 Bring a large saucepan of water to the boil. Drop in the gnocchi, 10–12 at a time, and poach them for 2–3 minutes or until they bob up to the surface. Remove with a draining spoon and drain well on kitchen paper. Transfer to a warmed ovenproof serving dish and keep warm in a low oven until all the gnocchi are cooked.

6 Meanwhile, gently warm the roasted pepper sauce over a low heat. Spoon the sauce over the gnocchi, garnish with sage leaves and serve.

Each serving provides
kcal 404, **protein** 18 g, **fat** 15 g (of which saturated fat 7 g), **carbohydrate** 52 g (of which sugars 11 g), **fibre** 5 g

✓✓✓	A, C, calcium
✓✓	B₁, E, zinc
✓	B₂, B₆, B₁₂, folate, niacin, copper, iron, potassium

Plus points

● Like other cheeses, ricotta is a good source of calcium. In addition, it offers good quantities of phosphorus, another mineral involved in ensuring bones and teeth are healthy. Phosphorus is also important in the release of energy from food.

● Pumpkin has a high water content, which makes it particularly low in calories – just 15 kcal per 100 g (3½ oz).

● Puréed vegetable sauces such as this are delicious low-fat dressings for pasta.

satisfying main dishes

Another idea

• For ricotta and fresh herb gnocchi, combine 250 g (8½ oz) ricotta cheese, 85 g (3 oz) finely chopped rocket, 20 g (¾ oz) finely chopped parsley, 3 tbsp snipped fresh chives, 1 beaten egg and 30 g (1 oz) freshly grated pecorino cheese. Add 200 g (7 oz) plain flour, 1 tsp freshly grated nutmeg, and salt and pepper to taste, and mix to a soft dough. Shape and cook as in the main recipe. Serve with a roasted tomato sauce: toss 500 g (1 lb 2 oz) small plum tomatoes and 2 garlic cloves in 1 tbsp extra virgin olive oil, then roast in a preheated 200°C (400°F, gas mark 6) oven for 20–25 minutes. Purée until smooth, and season to taste.

Spinach and smoked trout roulade

Flakes of smoked trout, creamy soft cheese and fresh dill combine to make a well-flavoured filling for this light spinach roll. It is much simpler to make than it looks – just make sure that the spinach is squeezed really dry before adding to the sauce base. Serve with a plum tomato salad and wholemeal rolls.

Serves 6

30 g (1 oz) cornmeal or polenta
200 g (7 oz) frozen leaf spinach, thawed
25 g (scant 1 oz) butter
25 g (scant 1 oz) plain flour
300 ml (10 fl oz) semi-skimmed milk
4 eggs, separated
pinch of freshly grated nutmeg
salt and pepper

Smoked trout filling

115 g (4 oz) reduced-fat soft cheese
4 tbsp fromage frais
2 tbsp chopped fresh dill
140 g (5 oz) skinless smoked trout fillet
2 tsp lemon juice

Plum tomato salad

1 tbsp extra virgin olive oil
2 tsp sherry vinegar
pinch of caster sugar
1 small onion, chopped
170 g (6 oz) baby plum tomatoes, halved

Preparation and cooking time: 40 minutes

Each serving provides

kcal 280, **protein** 17 g, **fat** 17 g (of which saturated fat 8 g), **carbohydrate** 14 g (of which sugars 7 g), **fibre** 1.5 g

✓✓✓	A, B$_{12}$
✓✓	calcium
✓	B$_1$, B$_2$, B$_6$, C, E, folate, niacin, iron, potassium, selenium, zinc

1 Lightly oil a 23 x 33 cm (9 x 13 in) Swiss roll tin and line with baking parchment. Sprinkle evenly with the cornmeal or polenta. Preheat the oven to 200°C (400°F, gas mark 6).

2 Squeeze the excess water out of the spinach, then chop finely. Melt the butter in a heavy-based saucepan, stir in the flour and cook for a few seconds. Off the heat, gradually whisk in the milk, then put back on a low heat and cook, whisking constantly, until the sauce bubbles and thickens. Remove from the heat and stir in the spinach, followed by the egg yolks, nutmeg, and salt and pepper to taste.

3 In a large clean bowl, whisk the egg whites until stiff. Fold into the spinach mixture, one-third at a time. Spoon into the prepared tin and gently level the surface.

4 Bake for 12–15 minutes or until slightly risen and firm to the touch. Place the tin on a wire rack, cover with a clean tea-towel and leave to cool for 5 minutes.

5 Meanwhile, make the filling. Put the soft cheese in a mixing bowl and mix in the fromage frais, 1 tbsp at a time. Stir in the dill, and season with salt and pepper to taste. Flake the trout into another bowl, and toss with the lemon juice.

6 Turn out the spinach 'cake' onto the tea-towel and carefully peel away the lining paper. Spread evenly with the soft cheese mixture, then arrange the smoked trout on top. Roll up the cake from one of the short ends. Transfer to a serving platter. (If making ahead of time, cover with cling film and keep in the fridge for up to 1 hour.)

7 For the plum tomato salad, whisk together the oil, vinegar, sugar and seasoning to taste in a bowl. Add the onion and toss to coat, then add the tomatoes and toss again.

8 Cut the roulade into 12 slices using an electric carving knife or a large serrated knife. Serve with the plum tomato salad.

Plus points

● Reduced-fat soft cheese provides essential nutrients such as protein and calcium. Its lower fat content means it has fewer calories than traditional cream cheese.

● Although spinach is a rich source of iron, the body is not able to absorb the iron easily. Serving a vitamin C-rich food such as tomatoes with the spinach helps to increase iron uptake.

satisfying main dishes

Another idea

● For a spinach and grilled pepper roulade, put 2 halved and seeded red or yellow peppers, cut side down, on a baking sheet with 2 unpeeled garlic cloves. Cook under a preheated hot grill for 10–12 minutes or until the peppers are blistered and blackened all over. Transfer to a polythene bag. When cool, peel the peppers and cut into thin strips. Squeeze the garlic pulp out of the skins and mix with the reduced-fat soft cheese and fromage frais. Instead of dill, add 1 tbsp each chopped fresh flat-leaf parsley and basil. Spread the cheese mixture over the cooled spinach 'cake', then scatter over the pepper strips. Roll up as in the main recipe.

Camembert and broccoli pancakes

Lacy, thin pancakes rolled around a tasty filling make a delightful main course. The beauty of this dish is that the pancakes, filling and tomato sauce topping can all be made in advance, then assembled and baked later. Serve with some crusty multigrain bread or boiled new potatoes, to boost the carbohydrate content.

Serves 4 (makes 8 pancakes)

115 g (4 oz) plain flour

2 eggs, beaten

250 ml (8½ fl oz) semi-skimmed milk

4 tsp sunflower oil

15 g (½ oz) Parmesan cheese, freshly grated

sprigs of fresh flat-leaf parsley to garnish

Tomato sauce

1 onion, chopped

1 garlic clove, chopped

1 can chopped tomatoes, about 400 g

pinch of sugar

2 tbsp chopped fresh flat-leaf parsley

Camembert and broccoli filling

250 g (8½ oz) broccoli, broken into tiny
    florets

150 g (5½ oz) Camembert cheese, diced

4 tbsp quark cheese

salt and pepper

Preparation time: 45 minutes

Cooking time: 25 minutes

Each serving provides

kcal 399, **protein** 27 g, **fat** 19 g (of which saturated fat 8 g), **carbohydrate** 34 g (of which sugars 10 g), **fibre** 4 g

✓✓✓	B₁₂, C, calcium
✓✓	B₂, E, folate, niacin, zinc
✓	A, B₁, B₆, copper, iron, potassium

1 First make the pancakes. Sift the flour into a bowl, add the eggs and a pinch of salt, and gradually whisk in the milk to form a smooth batter.

2 Brush an 18 cm (7 in) non-stick frying pan with a little of the oil, then heat. Add about one-eighth of the batter and tilt the pan so the batter coats the bottom thinly and evenly. Cook for about 45 seconds or until the pancake has set and the underside is lightly browned. Use a palette knife to loosen the edge of the pancake, then carefully turn it over and cook the other side for 30 seconds. Slide onto a plate.

3 Use the remaining batter to make 7 more pancakes, brushing the pan with more oil as necessary. Stack the cooked pancakes on the plate as they are made, interleaving them with greaseproof paper.

4 To make the tomato sauce, put the onion, garlic and tomatoes with their juice in a saucepan, and add the sugar, and salt and pepper to taste. Simmer for 10–15 minutes, stirring occasionally, until slightly thickened.

5 Meanwhile, make the filling. Cook the broccoli florets in boiling water for 4–5 minutes or until tender, then drain well. Tip into a bowl and add the Camembert, quark, and salt and pepper to taste. Fold together gently.

6 When the tomato sauce is cooked, remove from the heat and purée using a hand-held blender. Alternatively, leave to cool for 1–2 minutes, then pour into a food processor or blender to purée. Stir in the chopped parsley.

7 Preheat the oven to 200°C (400°F, gas mark 6). Divide the filling among the pancakes, roll them up and arrange side by side in an ovenproof dish. Pour over the tomato sauce to cover evenly and sprinkle with the Parmesan cheese. Bake for 25 minutes or until bubbling and golden brown. Garnish with parsley sprigs and serve.

Plus points

● Camembert and Brie are similar cheeses – both have a downy white rind and a soft, unctuous texture – but Camembert is smaller, and it is slightly lower in fat.

● Broccoli contains a number of disease-fighting phytochemicals, including indoles, which may help to protect against breast cancer. Indoles appear to inhibit the action of oestrogens that initiate tumour growth.

● Quark is a curd cheese from Germany. It is low in both fat and sodium.

Some more ideas

● The pancake batter can also be made in a food processor. Just put all the ingredients in the container and blend until smooth.

● Make up a double quantity of batter and prepare 16 pancakes, then freeze half for a later date. They will thaw at room temperature in about 2 hours.

● For Camembert and ratatouille pancakes, make a roasted ratatouille (see step 1, page 120), mix with the Camembert and use to fill the pancakes. Finish as in the main recipe.

● For Parma ham and broccoli pancakes, cook the broccoli as in the main recipe, then mix with 100 g (3½ oz) curd cheese. Trim all fat from 4 thin slices of Parma ham, about 50 g (1¾ oz) in total, and cut each slice in half. Place a piece of ham on each pancake, add the broccoli mixture and roll up. Arrange in an ovenproof dish and cover with a white sauce. To make the sauce, mix 1½ tbsp cornflour with a little semi-skimmed milk taken from 300 ml (10 fl oz). Heat the rest of the milk to boiling point. Stir into the cornflour mixture, then return to the pan and heat gently, stirring, until thickened. Simmer for 2 minutes. Add 1 tsp Dijon mustard, and salt and pepper to taste. Pour evenly over the pancakes and sprinkle with 55 g (2 oz) grated mature Gouda or other well-flavoured cheese. Bake as in the main recipe.

Haddock in egg and lemon sauce

Steaming fish atop vegetables and then using the cooking liquid to make a sauce is a good way to retain water-soluble vitamins. Here a piece of haddock fillet is cooked with baby carrots and courgettes, and the stock is then used to make the classic Greek egg and lemon sauce called avgolémono. A herb pilaf completes the meal.

Serves 4

600 ml (1 pint) fish stock

thinly pared strip of lemon zest

1 bay leaf

250 g (8½ oz) baby carrots

250 g (8½ oz) baby courgettes

450 g (1 lb) piece of haddock fillet, skinned and cut into 4 portions

2 tsp arrowroot

juice of 1 lemon

1 egg

Fresh herb pilaf

2 tsp extra virgin olive oil

15 g (½ oz) butter

225 g (8 oz) long-grain rice

600 ml (1 pint) boiling water

2 tbsp chopped fresh dill

1 tbsp chopped parsley

Preparation and cooking time: 35 minutes

Each serving provides

kcal 397, **protein** 29 g, **fat** 8 g (of which saturated fat 3 g), **carbohydrate** 56 g (of which sugars 5 g), **fibre** 2 g

✓✓✓	A, B$_6$, B$_{12}$, selenium
✓✓	B$_2$, C, niacin
✓	B$_1$, E, folate, calcium, copper, iron, potassium, zinc

1 First, start making the pilaf. Heat the oil and butter in a heavy-based saucepan, add the rice and fry gently for 2–3 minutes or until translucent. Slowly pour in the boiling water. Stir, then cover with a tight-fitting lid. Cook over a very low heat for 10–15 minutes or until the water has been absorbed and the rice is tender.

2 Meanwhile, put the fish stock in a saucepan with the lemon zest and bay leaf, and bring to the boil. Add the carrots, cover and simmer for 3 minutes. Add the courgettes. Place the haddock on top; it should be resting on the courgettes just above the stock. Cover and poach very gently for 7–8 minutes or until the fish is cooked through and the vegetables are tender.

3 Lift the cooked fish and vegetables out of the pan using a draining spoon and place on a plate. Cover and keep warm. Strain the stock and reserve 150 ml (5 fl oz) for the sauce.

4 Mix the arrowroot with the lemon juice in a small saucepan. Pour in the reserved stock and bring to the boil, stirring all the time until thickened.

5 Whisk the egg in a bowl, then pour in the hot stock mixture in a thin, steady stream, whisking constantly. Return to the pan and whisk over a low heat for about 3 minutes or until the

sauce is smooth and thick. Do not allow it to boil or the egg will curdle and spoil the texture. Season with salt and pepper to taste.

6 Place the fish on warmed plates with the vegetables. Spoon over the sauce. Fluff up the rice with a fork to separate the grains, then stir in the dill, parsley, and seasoning to taste. Serve the pilaf with the fish.

Plus points

- White fish such as haddock is an important source of good-quality protein, providing similar amounts to lean meat when judged on a weight for weight basis.
- Rice is an important crop all round the world, the staple of the diet of millions of people. In addition to starchy carbohydrates, rice is a source of protein, though less than other cereals, and of most of the B vitamins.
- Butter contains vitamins A, D and E. In contrast to other dairy products, it contains only a little calcium and no B vitamins.

Another idea

● For poached chicken with egg and coriander sauce, remove the skin from a 1.35 kg (3 lb) chicken, then put it into a deep saucepan in which it fits comfortably. Add 1 halved onion, 2 bay leaves and ½ tsp salt. Pour in enough water to cover. Bring to the boil, then cover and simmer very gently for 45 minutes, regularly skimming any froth from the surface. Add 675 g (1½ lb) scrubbed baby potatoes and simmer for a further 5 minutes, then add 250 g (8½ oz) baby leeks, cut into 5 cm (2 in) pieces. Simmer for about 10 more minutes or until the chicken is cooked, and the potatoes and leeks are tender. Transfer the chicken and vegetables to a warmed serving platter and keep warm. Blend 2 tsp arrowroot with 1 tbsp lemon juice in a small pan. Stir in 5 tbsp dry white wine and 120 ml (4 fl oz) of the chicken stock. Bring to the boil, stirring until thickened. Pour the sauce over 1 beaten egg in a bowl in a steady stream, whisking constantly. Return to the pan and whisk over a low heat for about 3 minutes or until smooth and thick. Stir in 3 tbsp chopped fresh coriander. Carve the chicken and serve with the vegetables and sauce. This dish needs no other accompaniments.

Gruyère gougère with ratatouille

Many cooks won't attempt to make a gougère, which is a choux pastry ring, because they think it's too difficult. However, nothing could be farther from the truth. Choux pastry is very simple to make, and it can be prepared ahead – shape the gougère and bake just before serving. The filling, too, can be made in advance.

Serves 4

Choux pastry

55 g (2 oz) butter

75 g (2½ oz) plain flour

2 eggs, beaten

55 g (2 oz) Gruyère cheese, finely grated

¼ tsp cayenne pepper

Roasted ratatouille filling

2 tbsp extra virgin olive oil

1 large aubergine, cut into 2 cm (¾ in) chunks

2 courgettes, cut into 2 cm (¾ in) chunks

1 red pepper, seeded and diced

1 green pepper, seeded and diced

1 onion, chopped

3 garlic cloves, finely chopped

1 can borlotti beans, about 410 g, drained and rinsed

1 can chopped tomatoes, about 400 g

3 tbsp chopped parsley

2 tbsp chopped fresh thyme

salt and pepper

Preparation and cooking time: about 1 hour

1 Preheat the oven to 220°C (425°F, gas mark 7). First make the roasted ratatouille. Drizzle the oil over the bottom of a large roasting tin, then add the aubergine, courgettes, red and green peppers, onion and garlic. Toss to coat the vegetables with the oil. Roast for 35–40 minutes or until golden brown and tender, turning the vegetables over after 20 minutes.

2 Meanwhile, make the choux pastry. Put the butter and 150 ml (5 fl oz) water in a saucepan. Heat gently until the butter has melted, then bring to the boil. As soon as the water boils, remove from the heat and quickly tip in the flour. Beat with a wooden spoon until the mixture forms a ball. Leave to cool for 2 minutes, then gradually beat in the eggs to make a smooth, stiff paste. Beat in the cheese and cayenne pepper.

3 Spoon the choux pastry evenly around the edge of a greased, shallow, 1.2 litre (2 pint) round or oval ovenproof dish. Put into the oven (still at the same temperature) and bake for about 25 minutes or until well risen and golden brown. (During the baking time, do not open the oven door.)

4 When the gougère is almost done, put the borlotti beans in a saucepan. Add the tomatoes with their juice, the parsley, chopped thyme, and salt and

pepper to taste. Cook over a low heat for about 5 minutes, stirring from time to time, until heated through.

5 Add the roasted vegetables to the bean mixture and stir gently to mix. Spoon this filling into the centre of the freshly baked gougère and serve.

Plus points

● Unlike many other foods, there are minimal losses of nutrients when cheese is cooked.

● Roasting vegetables brings out their full flavour and is a very low-fat method of cooking.

● Garlic is a source of the phytochemical allicin, believed to have both anti-fungal and antibiotic properties. Allicin is created when garlic is cut or smashed, and allicin produces the characteristic smell and taste. The more you chop garlic, the more pungent it will be.

Each serving provides Ⓥ

kcal 442, protein 17 g, fat 26 g (of which saturated fat 12 g), carbohydrate 37 g (of which sugars 13 g), fibre 8.5 g

✓✓✓	A, C
✓✓	B₁, B₆, B₁₂, E, folate, calcium, iron, potassium, zinc
✓	B₂, niacin, copper, selenium

satisfying main dishes

y

120

Some more ideas

• Make 4 large choux buns instead of a ring. Spoon the choux pastry into mounds on a lightly greased baking sheet. Bake for 15–20 minutes or until risen and golden brown. Split open and fill with the roasted ratatouille mixture.

• Replace the Gruyère with Emmenthal or fontina cheese, and the cayenne pepper with 4 thinly sliced spring onions and 2 tbsp chopped parsley.

• For leek and mushroom gougère, soften 1 thinly sliced leek in 1 tbsp sunflower oil, then add 500 g (1 lb 2 oz) thickly sliced chestnut mushrooms and 1 crushed garlic clove. Cook for a further 5 minutes or until the mushrooms are soft and have exuded their juices. Stir in 3 tbsp chopped parsley, 2 tbsp chopped fresh thyme and 1 can black-eyed beans, about 410 g, drained and rinsed. Season to taste. Heat through gently, then use to fill the freshly baked gougère.

Squash and taleggio risotto

This tasty risotto makes a tempting family meal. The combination of rice and fresh vegetables, gently cooked with white wine, stock and rosemary, then with creamy Italian taleggio cheese stirred in at the end, creates a nutritious dish packed with flavour. All you need is a leafy salad to complete the meal.

Serves 4

2 tbsp extra virgin olive oil

6 shallots, chopped

2 garlic cloves, crushed

500 g (1 lb 2 oz) butternut squash, peeled, seeded and diced

450 ml (15 fl oz) vegetable stock

225 g (8 oz) risotto rice

225 g (8 oz) chestnut mushrooms, sliced

250 ml (8½ fl oz) dry white wine

1 tbsp chopped fresh rosemary

225 g (8 oz) taleggio cheese, rinded and diced

salt and pepper

sprigs of fresh rosemary to garnish

Preparation time: 20 minutes
Cooking time: 35 minutes

Each serving provides 🅥

kcal 513, protein 18 g, fat 22 g (of which saturated fat 10 g), carbohydrate 50 g (of which sugars 5 g), fibre 2 g

✓✓✓	A, calcium
✓✓	niacin, zinc
✓	B₁, B₂, B₆, B₁₂, C, E, folate, copper, iron, potassium

1 Heat the oil in a large saucepan, add the shallots and garlic, and cook for 2 minutes or until the shallots begin to soften. Add the squash and cook for a further 10 minutes, stirring occasionally.

2 Meanwhile, put the vegetable stock into a saucepan and bring just to simmering point. Reduce the heat so the stock stays hot.

3 Add the rice to the squash and cook for 1 minute, stirring. Stir in the mushrooms, then add the wine and chopped rosemary. Bring just to the boil and bubble gently until most of the wine has been absorbed, stirring frequently.

4 Add a ladleful of the hot stock and simmer until it has been absorbed, stirring frequently. Continue gradually adding the stock in this way, waiting for each addition to be absorbed before adding more. When all the stock has been added, the rice should be tender but still firm and the risotto should have a creamy texture. Season with salt and pepper to taste.

5 Remove the risotto from the heat. Add the cheese and stir in gently until it starts to melt. Serve the risotto immediately, garnished with fresh rosemary sprigs.

Some more ideas

• Replace the shallots with 1 sliced leek.

• Instead of taleggio, use goat's cheese or a blue cheese such as Gorgonzola.

• For a fennel, courgette and pecorino risotto, cook 1 chopped onion, 2 chopped celery sticks and 2 crushed garlic cloves in 2 tbsp extra virgin olive oil for about 10 minutes or until softened. Stir in 350 g (12½ oz) sliced courgettes and 250 g (8½ oz) diced bulb fennel, and cook for 5 more minutes. Continue as in the main recipe, from step 2, but omitting the mushrooms. When the risotto has finished cooking, sprinkle over 115 g (4 oz) freshly grated pecorino cheese. Stir gently to mix into the risotto, then serve immediately.

Plus points

• Taleggio is an Italian cheese with a creamy consistency similar to Brie. Like other cheeses, it is a useful source of vitamin B₁₂. This vitamin is principally found in foods of animal origin, so for vegetarians cheese is an important food.

• The flavour of shallots tends to be milder and more subtle than that of onions. Like onions, shallots contain some vitamin C and B vitamins.

Smoked haddock soufflé

Light, fluffy soufflés rarely fail to impress, yet they are surprisingly easy to make. This recipe uses the fish-poaching milk to make the soufflé base, and fresh herbs and chopped tomatoes are added for a lovely flavour. Serve straight from the oven, with crusty wholemeal bread to accompany.

Serves 4

300 g (10½ oz) smoked haddock fillet

300 ml (10 fl oz) semi-skimmed milk

1 tsp butter

1 tbsp Parmesan cheese

1 tbsp fine dry breadcrumbs

3 tbsp cornflour

3 eggs, separated

250 g (8½ oz) tomatoes, skinned, seeded and diced

1 tsp wholegrain mustard

2 tbsp finely chopped parsley

2 tbsp finely snipped fresh chives

1 egg white

salt and pepper

Preparation time: about 35 minutes
Cooking time: 35 minutes

Each serving provides

kcal 250, **protein** 25 g, **fat** 9 g (of which saturated fat 3 g), **carbohydrate** 19 g (of which sugars 6 g), **fibre** 1 g

✓✓✓	B$_{12}$
✓✓	A, niacin, selenium
✓	B$_1$, B$_2$, B$_6$, C, E, folate, calcium, copper, iron, potassium, zinc

1 Put the haddock and milk in a saucepan and heat until simmering. Simmer gently for about 8 minutes or until the fish will just flake when tested with a fork. Remove the pan from the heat and leave the fish to cool in the milk. When the fish is cool enough to handle, remove it and flake the flesh, discarding the skin and any bones. Set the poaching milk aside to cool.

2 Preheat the oven, with a metal baking sheet inside, to 190°C (375°F, gas mark 5). Lightly grease a 1.7 litre (3 pint) soufflé dish with the butter. Mix together the Parmesan and breadcrumbs, and sprinkle over the bottom and side of the dish, turning the dish to coat evenly. Shake out any excess crumb mixture and reserve.

3 Mix the cornflour with a little of the reserved, cold poaching milk to make a smooth paste. Heat the remaining milk in a small saucepan until almost boiling, then pour into the cornflour mixture, stirring constantly. Return to the pan and bring to the boil, stirring to make a thick sauce.

4 Pour the sauce into a large mixing bowl. Add the egg yolks, one by one, beating them thoroughly into the sauce. Stir in the flaked haddock, tomatoes, mustard, parsley, chives, and salt and pepper to taste.

5 In a clean, dry mixing bowl, whisk the 4 egg whites until stiff enough to hold soft peaks. Fold one-quarter of the whites into the sauce mixture to lighten it, then gently fold in the remaining whites.

6 Spoon the mixture into the prepared soufflé dish and sprinkle the top with the reserved Parmesan and breadcrumb mixture. Set the dish on the hot baking sheet and bake for about 35 minutes or until well risen and golden brown. Serve at once.

Plus points

• Haddock is a useful source of vitamin B$_6$. This vitamin helps the body to make use of protein from food and to form haemoglobin, the pigment in red blood cells.

• Milk is an excellent source of many essential nutrients, the majority of which are concentrated in the non-fat part of milk. Semi-skimmed and skimmed milk therefore contain more of these nutrients than full-fat milks.

• Thickening the soufflé base with cornflour, instead of the more traditional method using butter, helps to reduce the total fat content of this recipe.

Another idea

• To make a Mediterranean-style goat's cheese soufflé, put 55 g (2 oz) dry-packed sun-dried tomatoes in a small bowl and pour over boiling water to cover. Leave to soak for 30 minutes, then drain and finely chop. In step 3, make the thick sauce base with 3 tbsp cornflour and 300 ml (10 fl oz) semi-skimmed milk. After beating in the egg yolks, add 100 g (3½ oz) creamy goat's cheese and beat until smooth. Stir in the sun-dried tomatoes and the herbs, and season with salt and pepper to taste. Fold in the stiffly whisked egg whites, then spoon the mixture into the soufflé dish. Finish and bake as in the main recipe.

Creamy curried eggs

A coconut curry sauce goes beautifully with eggs, and an aromatic vegetable pilaf is perfect alongside. Finish with some vitamin C-rich fruit, such as sliced mangoes, to ensure maximum absorption of iron from the eggs.

Serves 4

20 g (¾ oz) unsalted butter

1 small onion, very finely chopped

1 garlic clove, crushed

1 tbsp curry paste

1 can chopped tomatoes, about 200 g

90 ml (3 fl oz) coconut milk

2 tbsp chopped fresh coriander

8 eggs, at room temperature

Cauliflower and pea pilaf

1 tbsp sunflower oil

170 g (6 oz) small cauliflower florets

1 fresh red chilli, seeded and very finely chopped

1 cinnamon stick, halved

4 whole cloves

1 bay leaf

250 g (8½ oz) basmati rice

600 ml (1 pint) vegetable stock

150 g (5½ oz) frozen peas

salt and pepper

sprigs of fresh coriander to garnish

Preparation and cooking time: 45 minutes

Each serving provides ⓥ

kcal 528, **protein** 25 g, **fat** 22 g (of which saturated fat 7 g), **carbohydrate** 59 g (of which sugars 6 g), **fibre** 3 g

✓✓✓	A, B$_{12}$
✓✓	B$_2$, C, E, folate, niacin, iron, zinc
✓	B$_1$, B$_6$, calcium, copper, potassium, selenium

1 Melt the butter in a non-stick saucepan and gently fry the onion for 7–8 minutes or until softened. Stir in the garlic and curry paste, and cook for a further 1 minute. Add the chopped tomatoes with their juice and simmer for 10 minutes or until fairly thick. Stir in the coconut milk and simmer for a further 5 minutes. Add the chopped coriander, and season with salt and pepper to taste. Cover and keep warm.

2 To make the pilaf, heat the oil in a heavy-based saucepan, add the cauliflower florets and cook over a moderate heat for 1–2 minutes, stirring frequently, until just beginning to colour. Stir in the chilli, cinnamon stick, cloves and bay leaf, and cook for a further 30 seconds.

3 Add the rice and stir well to mix with the vegetables and spices. Pour in the stock. Bring to the boil, then reduce the heat, cover and simmer gently for 5 minutes. Stir in the peas, cover the pan again and cook for a further 7–10 minutes or until the rice is tender and all the stock has been absorbed. Season with salt and pepper to taste.

4 While the pilaf is cooking, hard-boil the eggs. Put them into a saucepan and cover with tepid water. Bring to the boil, then reduce the heat and simmer for 7 minutes. Remove the eggs with a draining spoon and place in a bowl of cold water. When they are cool enough to handle, peel off their shells and cut them in half lengthways.

5 Arrange the egg halves on warmed serving plates and spoon over the coconut sauce. Serve with the pilaf, removing the bay leaf and whole spices first, if preferred. Garnish with sprigs of fresh coriander.

Plus points

● Iron is found in ground spices such as cumin, cardamom and turmeric. The amount is small, but if spices are used regularly in cooking, the iron intake can start to add up.

● Canned tomatoes are a very useful and nutritious item for the storecupboard. The antioxidant lycopene in tomatoes is enhanced by cooking, so processed products such as canned tomatoes, tomato purée and ketchup are better sources than fresh tomatoes.

satisfying main dishes

Some more ideas

- Use quail's eggs, allowing 5 per person. Cooking time is 1–2 minutes. Increase the peas in the pilaf to 250 g (8½ oz).
- For quick creamy curried eggs, heat 1 tsp sunflower oil in a small saucepan and stir in 1 tbsp curry paste. Cook for 1 minute, then stir in 115 g (4 oz) curd cheese, 6 tbsp coconut milk and 1 tbsp smooth mango chutney. Cook over a low heat, stirring constantly, until the mixture is smooth and hot, then add 1 tbsp chopped fresh coriander, and season with salt and pepper to taste. Spoon over the halved hard-boiled eggs and serve with plain boiled basmati rice or warm naan bread.

Sweet Finales

New ways with puddings

Many favourite puddings and desserts are made with eggs and dairy products. Traditional recipes can be high in fat and calories, but it's easy to prepare healthier versions that are just as delicious. Bake little vanilla custards and top them with a fresh cherry compote. Simmer pudding rice in sweetened milk, then serve hot with cinnamon-spiced apricots. Make citrus and quark cheese soufflés or a light, sweet soufflé omelette filled with apples and blackberries. Layer a mix of whipped cream and yogurt with dried peach and prune purées. Float poached meringues on a custard lake and drizzle with a blueberry sauce. Or make a frozen berry yogurt.

Quark citrus soufflés

These deliciously light, individual citrus soufflés will be a tempting and refreshing end to any meal. Quark is low in fat and provides valuable nutrients such as calcium without adding too many calories. The accompanying strawberry coulis looks pretty and complements the soufflés perfectly, as well as contributing vitamin C.

Serves 6

15 g (½ oz) unsalted butter, melted

115 g (4 oz) caster sugar

4 eggs, separated

30 g (1 oz) cornflour

250 g (8½ oz) quark cheese

finely grated zest of 1 lime

finely grated zest of 1 small orange

sifted icing sugar to dust

Strawberry coulis

300 g (10½ oz) ripe strawberries, halved

2 tsp icing sugar, or to taste, sifted

dash of liqueur, such as kirsch (optional)

Preparation time: 30 minutes

Cooking time: 15–20 minutes

1 Preheat the oven to 190°C (375°F, gas mark 5). Brush 6 individual 200 ml (7 fl oz) soufflé dishes with the melted butter, then coat with caster sugar, using 30 g (1 oz) sugar in total. Set the dishes aside.

2 Put the egg yolks, 30 g (1 oz) of the caster sugar and the cornflour in a bowl and whisk together until creamy. Add the quark and the lime and orange zests, and whisk until thoroughly mixed.

3 In a clean mixing bowl, whisk the egg whites until stiff. Gradually whisk in the remaining 55 g (2 oz) caster sugar. Carefully fold the whisked egg whites into the quark mixture.

4 Spoon the mixture into the prepared soufflé dishes and set them on a baking sheet. Bake for 15–20 minutes or until well risen and golden brown.

5 Meanwhile, make the strawberry coulis. Purée the strawberries in a blender or food processor until smooth. Sweeten with the icing sugar, then stir in the liqueur, if using.

6 Serve the hot soufflés straight from the oven, dusted with a little icing sugar and with the coulis alongside.

Some more ideas

● Instead of flavouring the soufflés with lime and orange zests, try lemon and orange, or pink grapefruit and orange.

● Coat the buttered dishes with 15 g (½ oz) finely crushed macaroons or ground hazelnuts instead of caster sugar.

● For a mixed berry soufflé, grease a 1.7 litre (3 pint) soufflé dish with melted unsalted butter and dust with caster sugar. Make the soufflé mixture as in the main recipe, flavouring with the finely grated zest of 1 lemon and 1 lime. Put 350 g (12½ oz) mixed berries, such as raspberries, strawberries and blackberries, into the prepared soufflé dish. Spoon the soufflé mixture over the fruit, covering it completely, and bake for 30 minutes or until well risen and golden brown. Dust with sifted icing sugar and serve immediately.

Plus points

● Quark is a soft curd cheese that can be made from skimmed or full-fat milk or from buttermilk. The fat content can therefore vary from low to virtually fat-free.

● Eggs are a good source of zinc, a mineral that is vital for growth, reproduction and efficient working of the immune system.

Each serving provides   Ⓥ

kcal 221, **protein** 12 g, **fat** 7 g (of which saturated fat 2 g), **carbohydrate** 31 g (of which sugars 27 g), **fibre** 0.5 g

✓✓	B₁₂, C
✓	A, B₂, folate, niacin, calcium, copper, zinc

Rice pudding with apricots

Rich in flavour and wonderfully creamy in texture, this satisfying rice pudding is a modern version of a popular old favourite. It's flavoured with tangy orange zest and sultanas, and paired with a cinnamon-spiced fresh apricot compote, to make a delicious dessert that is suitable both for family meals and for entertaining.

Serves 4

850 ml (1 pint + 8½ fl oz) full-fat milk

45 g (1½ oz) caster sugar

finely grated zest of 1 orange

100 g (3½ oz) short-grain 'pudding' rice

55 g (2 oz) sultanas

ground cinnamon to sprinkle

Apricot compote

300 g (10½ oz) fresh ripe apricots, halved and stoned

juice of 1 orange

1 cinnamon stick

Preparation time: 15 minutes

Cooking time: about 1¼ hours

Each serving provides

kcal 334, protein 9 g, fat 8 g (of which saturated fat 5 g), carbohydrate 59 g (of which sugars 37 g), fibre 2 g

✓✓	A, B₁₂, calcium
✓	B₁, B₂, B₆, C, niacin, copper, potassium, zinc

1 Preheat the oven to 160°C (325°F, gas mark 3). Pour the milk into a saucepan, and add the sugar and orange zest. Heat gently, stirring, until the sugar dissolves and the milk is almost boiling.

2 Put the rice and sultanas in a shallow 1.5 litre (2¾ pint) ovenproof dish. Pour over the milk mixture and stir.

3 Bake the pudding for 30 minutes, then stir well. Leave to bake for a further 45 minutes or until the rice is tender and the pudding is creamy.

4 Meanwhile, to make the compote, combine the apricots, orange juice and cinnamon stick in a heavy-based saucepan. Cover and cook over a low heat for 10 minutes. Remove the lid and cook for a further 5 minutes or until the juice is reduced.

5 Remove the cinnamon stick from the compote. Sprinkle the top of the rice pudding with a little cinnamon, then serve hot, with the compote.

Some more ideas

● Cook the rice pudding as in the main recipe, then leave to cool completely. When cold, spoon into 4 lightly oiled, individual moulds or teacups, packing the pudding down firmly. Chill for about 1 hour, then turn out carefully onto serving plates. Serve with the chilled apricot compote.

● Make a sweet semolina pudding with a plum compote. Heat 850 ml (1 pint + 8½ fl oz) milk with 2 tbsp clear honey and a thinly pared strip of lemon zest. Stir in 100 g (3½ oz) semolina. Stir until boiling, then add 55 g (2 oz) sultanas and reduce the heat so the mixture is just simmering. Cover the pan and simmer gently, stirring occasionally, for 20–25 minutes or until thick and smooth. To make the plum compote, combine 300 g (10½ oz) red plums, the juice of 1 orange and 1 tsp finely grated fresh root ginger in a heavy-based saucepan, and cook gently, covered, for about 20 minutes or until the plums are very tender.

Plus points

● Dried fruit is naturally sweet, so using it in a pudding means the sugar can be reduced to a minimum.

● The combination of rice and milk works well nutritionally. Rice is a good source of starchy carbohydrate, fibre, B vitamins and iron, and milk is a good source of protein and calcium. As full-fat milk is used in this recipe, the fat-soluble vitamin A is also supplied.

sweet finales

Little custard pots

These creamy baked custards, delicately flavoured with vanilla and accompanied by a fresh cherry compote, are easy to make and sure to be popular with all ages. Take care not to overcook the custards – they should be just set when you take them out of the oven. This dessert can be prepared well ahead of serving.

Serves 6

600 ml (1 pint) semi-skimmed milk

½ vanilla pod, split

2 eggs

2 egg yolks

40 g (1¼ oz) caster sugar

½ tsp cornflour

Cherry compote

30 g (1 oz) demerara sugar

450 g (1 lb) fresh cherries, stoned

2 tsp arrowroot

Preparation time: 15 minutes
Cooking time: 25–30 minutes

Each serving provides Ⓥ

kcal 188, **protein** 7 g, **fat** 6 g (of which saturated fat 2 g), **carbohydrate** 29 g (of which sugars 26 g), **fibre** 1 g

✓✓	B₁₂
✓	A, B₂, C, calcium, zinc

1 Place the milk and vanilla pod in a saucepan and heat until almost boiling. Remove from the heat, cover and set aside to infuse for 15 minutes.

2 Preheat the oven to 160°C (325°F, gas mark 3). Put the whole eggs, egg yolks, caster sugar and cornflour into a bowl and lightly whisk together.

3 Bring the milk back to boiling point, then remove the vanilla pod and pour the hot milk over the egg mixture, whisking all the time. Strain the mixture into a jug, then divide among 6 lightly buttered 120 ml (4 fl oz) ramekin dishes.

4 Set the ramekins in a roasting tin and pour enough hot water into the tin to come halfway up the sides of the ramekins. Bake for 30–35 minutes or until lightly set – the custards should still be slightly wobbly, as they will continue cooking for a few minutes after being removed from the oven. Lift them out of the tin of hot water and place on a wire rack to cool. Once cold, chill until ready to serve.

5 For the cherry compote, put the demerara sugar and 6 tbsp water in a saucepan and heat gently until the sugar has dissolved. Bring to the boil, then reduce the heat and add the cherries. Cover and simmer gently for 4–5 minutes, stirring occasionally, until tender. Lift out the cherries with a draining spoon and put them into a serving bowl.

6 Mix the arrowroot with 1 tbsp cold water. Stir into the cherry juices in the saucepan and simmer for 1 minute, stirring, until thickened and clear. Allow to cool for a few minutes, then pour over the cherries. (The compote can be served warm or at room temperature.)

7 Spoon a little of the cherry compote over the top of each custard pot, and serve the rest of the compote in a bowl.

Plus points

● Adding extra egg yolks in this recipe boosts the content of vitamins A and D and most of the B vitamins, as these nutrients are concentrated in the yolk of the egg rather than the white.

● Cherries are rich in potassium and provide useful amounts of vitamin C.

Some more ideas

• If you want to turn out the custards for serving, line the bottom of each ramekin with a circle of baking parchment, and add an extra egg yolk to the mixture. After baking, chill for at least 4 hours or, preferably, overnight. To turn out, lightly press the edge of each custard with your fingertips to pull it away from the dish, then run a knife around the edge. Put an inverted serving plate on top of the ramekin, then turn them both over, holding them firmly together, and lift off the ramekin.

• For chocolate custard pots with poached pears, flavour the milk with a thin strip of pared orange zest instead of the vanilla pod. In step 2, replace the caster sugar with light soft brown sugar, and add 1 tbsp sifted cocoa powder. Continue making the custards as in the main recipe. For the pears, heat 300 ml (10 fl oz) water with 85 g (3 oz) caster sugar and a split vanilla pod until the sugar dissolves, then bring to the boil and simmer for 2–3 minutes. Add 4 small, firm dessert pears, peeled, cored and thickly sliced. Cover and simmer gently for 12–15 minutes or until just tender, turning the pear slices in the syrup occasionally. Lift out the pears with a draining spoon and transfer to a serving dish. Simmer the syrup for 5 minutes to reduce slightly, then cool for 5 minutes. Remove the vanilla pod and pour over the pears.

sweet finales

Monmouth pudding

Here a nursery-style pudding, popular in Victorian times, is given a new look with fresh raspberries rather than the traditional jam. The texture of the pudding is beautifully light due to the addition of fresh breadcrumbs and whisked egg whites. Served with a fresh raspberry sauce, this is sure to become a family favourite.

Serves 4

200 ml (7 fl oz) semi-skimmed milk

200 g (7 oz) fresh white breadcrumbs, preferably made from day-old bread

20 g (¾ oz) unsalted butter, softened and diced

grated zest of 1 lemon

125 g (4½ oz) raspberries

85 g (3 oz) caster sugar

2 eggs, separated

1 egg white

sifted icing sugar to dust

Raspberry sauce

125 g (4½ oz) raspberries

1 tbsp icing sugar, sifted

Preparation time: 25 minutes
Cooking time: 40–45 minutes

1 Preheat the oven to 140°C (275°F, gas mark 1). Heat the milk until scalding hot, but not quite boiling. Put the breadcrumbs into a large, heatproof bowl and pour over the hot milk. Stir in the butter and lemon zest, then leave to cool for 10–15 minutes or until the crumbs have absorbed the milk.

2 Meanwhile, put the raspberries in a mixing bowl. Sprinkle over 30 g (1 oz) of the caster sugar and mash with a fork to make a thick, rough mixture. Spread over the bottom of a lightly buttered 1.2 litre (2 pint) baking dish.

3 Stir the egg yolks into the cooled breadcrumb mixture. Put the 3 egg whites into a clean bowl and whisk until stiff peaks form, then whisk in the remaining 55 g (2 oz) caster sugar. With a large metal spoon, gently fold the egg whites into the breadcrumb mixture.

4 Spoon the breadcrumb mixture on top of the raspberries. Bake for 40–45 minutes or until the pudding is set and lightly golden.

5 Meanwhile, make the sauce. Purée the raspberries by pressing them through a nylon sieve. Stir in the icing sugar, then pour into a serving jug.

6 Remove the pudding from the oven and leave to cool slightly, then dust the top with icing sugar. Serve warm, with the raspberry sauce.

Some more ideas

● Serve with 2 tbsp plain low-fat bio yogurt per person as well as the raspberry sauce.

● For college pudding, another Victorian nursery favourite, pour 100 ml (3½ fl oz) hot semi-skimmed milk over 100 g (3½ oz) slightly stale wholemeal breadcrumbs. Add 100 g (3½ oz) mixed sultanas and raisins, plus ½ tsp each freshly grated nutmeg, ground allspice and ground cinnamon. Stir in 2 tbsp caster sugar and 75 g (2½ oz) softened unsalted butter. Leave to cool for 10 minutes, then stir in 1 egg, lightly beaten, and ½ tsp baking powder. Spoon into a buttered 600 ml (1 pint) pudding basin, cover tightly with a piece of buttered foil and steam in a pan of simmering water for about 1½ hours or until set. Turn out and serve with the raspberry sauce.

Plus points

● Egg whites contain no fat or cholesterol but do contain protein. They are therefore particularly useful for those who need to follow a very low-fat diet.

● Raspberries are an excellent source of vitamin C as well as containing useful amounts of folate and fibre.

Each serving provides ⓥ

kcal 339, **protein** 11 g, **fat** 9 g (of which saturated fat 4 g), **carbohydrate** 56 g (of which sugars 33 g), **fibre** 2 g

✓✓	B$_{12}$, C, selenium
✓	A, B$_1$, B$_2$, folate, niacin, calcium, copper, iron, zinc

Apple-berry soufflé omelette

This light, sweet omelette should be cooked just before serving, but can be prepared up to the end of step 2 an hour ahead. It's a simple yet delectable pudding to make in late summer/early autumn.

Serves 2

2 crisp dessert apples, such as Cox's
55 g (2 oz) blackberries
½ tsp ground allspice
1½ tbsp caster sugar
2 eggs, separated
finely grated zest of ½ orange
½ tsp pure vanilla extract
15 g (½ oz) unsalted butter
1 tsp demerara sugar
2 tbsp Greek-style yogurt

Preparation time: 15 minutes
Cooking time: 5–8 minutes

Each serving provides

kcal 309, **protein** 10 g, **fat** 16 g (of which saturated fat 8 g), **carbohydrate** 33 g (of which sugars 33 g), **fibre** 3 g

✓✓✓	B$_{12}$
✓✓	A
✓	B$_2$, C, E, folate, niacin, calcium, copper, iron, selenium, zinc

1 Peel, core and thickly slice the apples. Put into a small saucepan and add the blackberries, allspice and 1 tbsp of the caster sugar. Cover and heat gently for 2–3 minutes, shaking the pan occasionally, until the fruit juices run and the sugar has dissolved. Remove from the heat and keep warm.

2 Put the egg yolks, remaining ½ tbsp caster sugar, the orange zest and vanilla extract in a bowl, and whisk together until smooth and thick.

3 In a separate, clean bowl, whisk the egg whites until they form soft peaks. Using a large metal spoon, fold the whites into the yolk mixture.

4 Preheat the grill to moderately hot. Melt the butter in a 20 cm (8 in) frying pan with a heatproof handle. Tip in the egg mixture, spreading it evenly, and cook gently for 2–3 minutes or until set and golden on the base.

5 Place the pan under the grill and cook for 1–2 minutes or until the omelette is puffed up and just set on top. Remove from the heat and turn up the grill to high.

6 Spoon the fruit mixture on top of the omelette and fold it over in half. Sprinkle with the demerara sugar and grill for about 30 seconds or until the sugar caramelises. Cut the omelette in half and serve immediately, topped with the yogurt.

Some more ideas

● For a cherry soufflé omelette, replace the apples and blackberries with 150 g (5½ oz) stoned red cherries. Poach with 1 tbsp caster sugar and a star anise or bay leaf until the juices run. Make the omelette as in the main recipe, but replacing the vanilla extract with pure almond extract.

● Make a caramelised apple soufflé omelette. Melt 15 g (½ oz) unsalted butter, add 2 sliced dessert apples and sprinkle with 15 g (½ oz) light soft brown sugar. Sauté for 4–5 minutes, stirring, until tender and caramelised. Sprinkle with the grated zest of 1 lemon, then use to fill the omelette made as in the main recipe.

Plus points

● Blackberries and other blue or purple-coloured fruits get their colour from flavonoids, powerful antioxidants that help to protect against coronary heart disease.

● The use of dessert apples instead of a cooking variety means that they need only light cooking and therefore not only retain their shape and texture but also much of their nutritive value too.

● The sodium content of unsalted butter is only 11 mg per 100 g (3½ oz), compared with salted butter which has a content of 750 mg per 100 g (3½ oz).

Marbled winter fruit fool

Dried prunes and peaches have an intense, concentrated flavour and sweetness and, with the addition of a dash of peach schnapps or brandy, they make a really special fruit fool. This is an attractive dessert for the winter months, when soft fruits for fools are not in season, and it's healthily modest in fat content.

Serves 4

150 g (5½ oz) ready-to-eat dried peaches
150 g (5½ oz) ready-to-eat stoned prunes
2 tbsp peach schnapps or brandy
200 ml (7 fl oz) orange juice, or as needed
150 ml (5 fl oz) whipping cream
150 g (5½ oz) plain low-fat yogurt

Preparation and cooking time: 30 minutes

1 Cut 30 g (1 oz) of the peaches and 30 g (1 oz) of the prunes into small dice. Put into a bowl, pour over the schnapps or brandy, and set aside to marinate.

2 Place the remaining peaches and prunes in 2 separate saucepans and pour 100 ml (3½ fl oz) orange juice into each. Bring to the boil, then reduce the heat and simmer gently for 10 minutes or until the fruit is tender.

3 Purée the peaches and prunes separately in a blender or food processor until smooth, adding a little extra orange juice if needed.

4 Whip the cream in a mixing bowl until thick. Add the yogurt and whip to mix with the cream.

5 Layer alternate spoonfuls of the peach purée, prune purée and cream mixture into 4 stemmed glasses, swirling slightly for a marbled effect. Spoon the marinated fruits on top just before serving.

Some more ideas

• Use extra orange juice instead of the peach schnapps or brandy.

• For a rhubarb fool, cook 300 g (10½ oz) chopped rhubarb with 2 tbsp caster sugar and 1 tbsp orange juice. Cool, then purée. Make the cream and yogurt mixture as in the main recipe, then lightly swirl in the rhubarb purée. Spoon

into individual glasses or dishes. Decorate with 15 g (½ oz) toasted flaked almonds.

• To make a plum fool, halve and stone 300 g (10½ oz) red plums and poach gently in a covered pan with 15 g (½ oz) caster sugar and 1 tbsp orange juice until tender. Cool, then purée until smooth. Beat together 200 g (7 oz) fromage frais and 100 g (3½ oz) plain low-fat bio yogurt. Reserve 4 tbsp of the plum purée, then swirl the rest with the fromage frais mixture in stemmed glasses. Top each with a spoonful of the reserved purée and decorate with 15 g (½ oz) chopped toasted hazelnuts.

Plus points

• Dried fruits are a concentrated source of many nutrients, including iron. The vitamin C in the orange juice aids the absorption of iron from the dried fruits.

• Mixing low-fat yogurt with whipped cream produces a rich-tasting dessert that is delightfully low in calories. The yogurt also adds a pleasant hint of sharpness to contrast with the sweet fruit purée.

Each serving provides Ⓥ

kcal 320, **protein** 5 g, **fat** 15.5 g (of which saturated fat 9 g), **carbohydrate** 40 g (of which sugars 40 g), **fibre** 4.5 g

✓✓	A, C
✓	B₂, niacin, calcium, copper, iron, zinc

sweet finales

Pannacotta

The traditional recipe for this 'cooked cream', from the Piedmont region of Italy, is made with rich double cream. This lighter version, served with a pretty rhubarb and strawberry compote, is delightfully smooth and creamy yet much lower in fat. Prepare it the day before serving, if possible.

Serves 4

500 ml (17 fl oz) semi-skimmed milk

1 tbsp powdered gelatine

75 g (2½ oz) caster sugar

100 ml (3½ fl oz) single cream

strip of pared orange zest

1 vanilla pod, split

Rhubarb and strawberry compote

400 g (14 oz) pink rhubarb, trimmed and cut into 5 cm (2 in) lengths

juice of 1 orange

30 g (1 oz) caster sugar

450 g (1 lb) ripe strawberries, sliced

Preparation and cooking time: 30 minutes, plus at least 3 hours chilling

Each serving provides

kcal 265, **protein** 10 g, **fat** 7 g (of which saturated fat 4 g), **carbohydrate** 43 g (of which sugars 43 g), **fibre** 3 g

✓✓✓	C
✓✓	calcium
✓	A, B₂, B₁₂, folate, copper, potassium, zinc

1 Pour 150 ml (5 fl oz) of the milk into a saucepan. Sprinkle over the gelatine and leave to soak, without stirring, for 5 minutes or until spongy.

2 Stir in the sugar, then set the pan over a low heat. Warm gently, without boiling, until the sugar and gelatine have completely dissolved, stirring frequently.

3 Remove the pan from the heat and add the remaining milk, the cream and orange zest. Scrape the seeds from the vanilla pod into the milk mixture, then add the pod too. Leave to infuse for 10 minutes while preparing the compote.

4 Place the rhubarb in a saucepan with the orange juice and sugar. Bring just to a simmer, then cook gently for 3–4 minutes or until the rhubarb is tender but still holding its shape. Spoon the rhubarb into a serving dish using a draining spoon. Boil the juice remaining in the pan to reduce it slightly until syrupy. Pour the juice over the rhubarb and gently stir in the sliced strawberries. Leave to cool.

5 Strain the milk mixture through a fine sieve into a jug, then pour into 4 moulds, cups or ramekins of 170 ml (6 fl oz) capacity. Allow to cool, then cover and chill for at least 3 hours or until set.

6 To serve, run the tip of a knife around the edge of each pannacotta. Place an inverted serving plate over the top of the ramekin and turn them upside down, holding the two firmly together. Lift off the ramekin. Spoon some of the compote on the side of the pannacotta. Serve the remaining compote separately.

Plus points

● A fruit compote complements a creamy dessert in taste and colour, and also adds nutritional benefits.

● Although used as a fruit, rhubarb is actually a vegetable. It contains vitamin C and is a good source of potassium.

● Soft fruits such as strawberries are rich in vitamin C and contain useful amounts of potassium.

Some more ideas

• If you do not have a vanilla pod, use a few drops of pure vanilla extract.

• Serve the pannacotta with a fresh raspberry sauce (see Monmouth pudding, page 136).

• For rosewater pannacotta, instead of orange zest and vanilla, add 1 tsp rosewater and the seeds from 8 cardamom pods to the milk and cream mixture in step 2, then leave to infuse. Serve with a fresh raspberry and passion fruit sauce. To make the sauce, push 450 g (1 lb) raspberries through a fine sieve, then mix the purée with 1 tbsp sifted icing sugar and the juice of ½ orange. Stir in the pulp scooped from 2 passion fruits.

Ginger-glazed pears stuffed with ricotta and rum raisins

This simple dessert tastes just as delicious as it looks. After brushing with a honey, lemon and ginger syrup, the hollowed-out pears are filled with rum-soaked raisins and ricotta. Low in both fat and calories, this is the perfect way to turn the classic combination of fresh fruit and cheese into something a bit special.

Serves 4

50 g (1¾ oz) raisins

1 tbsp dark rum

170 g (6 oz) ricotta cheese

30 g (1 oz) preserved stem ginger in syrup, drained and finely chopped

3 large, firm but ripe dessert pears

2 tsp thick clear honey

1 tsp lemon juice

3 tbsp ginger syrup (from the jar of stem ginger)

sprigs of fresh mint to decorate

Preparation and cooking time: 35–40 minutes, plus 2 hours soaking and cooling

Each serving provides　Ⓥ

kcal 224, **protein** 5 g, **fat** 5 g (of which saturated fat 3 g), **carbohydrate** 41 g (of which sugars 41 g), **fibre** 3 g

✓　A, C, calcium, copper, potassium, zinc

1　Put the raisins in a small mixing bowl. Spoon over the rum and leave to soak for at least 2 hours or until the raisins are plump and have soaked up all the rum.

2　Add the ricotta and chopped stem ginger to the soaked raisins and mix well. Set aside. Preheat the grill to moderate.

3　Quarter the pears lengthways. Peel them, then scoop out the core with a teaspoon to make a cavity in each quarter. Arrange the pear quarters on their sides on the rack of the grill pan.

4　Mix together the honey, lemon juice and ginger syrup, and brush all over the pears. Grill for 4–6 minutes or until just tinged with colour. Turn and cook the other sides for 2–3 minutes.

5　Turn the pears cavity side up and brush again with the syrup mixture. Divide the ricotta and raisin mixture among the pear cavities, mounding the mixture up slightly. Make sure that the raisins aren't exposed, or they may burn during grilling.

6　Return the pears to the grill and cook for a further 3–4 minutes or until the filling is lightly browned. Leave to cool.

7　To serve, arrange the stuffed pears on serving plates. Drizzle over the remaining syrup mixture and decorate with sprigs of fresh mint.

Plus points

● Raisins contain useful amounts of fibre, iron and potassium as well as natural sugar. They are also virtually fat-free.

● In herbal medicine, ginger is believed to have special properties that can aid digestion, protect against infections in the respiratory and digestive systems, and also relieve flatulence.

sweet finales

144

Some more ideas

● Instead of rum, soak the raisins in orange liqueur or orange juice.

● Replace the raisins with other dried fruit such as finely chopped mango, apricots or pineapple.

● Make pashka, a ricotta and dried fruit dessert traditionally served at the end of Lent in Russia. Put 115 g (4 oz) chopped, ready-to-eat dried fruits, such as apricots and raisins, in a bowl with the finely grated zest and juice of 1 lemon and 1 tsp pure vanilla extract. Stir, then cover and leave to soak for 1 hour. Line a 13 cm (5½ in) clean plastic flowerpot (with draining holes) with a double layer of muslin, allowing the muslin to hang over the sides of the pot. Add 450 g (1 lb) ricotta cheese, 150 ml (5 fl oz) soured cream, 30 g (1 oz) caster sugar, 40 g (1¼ oz) clear honey and 55 g (2 oz) chopped blanched almonds to the soaked fruits. Mix well, then spoon into the flowerpot. Fold over the edges of the muslin, cover with a small saucer that fits inside the flowerpot and place a weight on top. Stand the flowerpot in a bowl and chill overnight. Unfold the muslin, turn the pashka out onto a plate and remove the muslin. Serve with a cherry compote (see Little custard pots, page 134). This will serve 6–8.

Strawberry yogurt mousse

This lovely strawberry dessert captures the taste of summer. Creamy, mild bio yogurt is used in place of cream for a lighter, lower fat mousse, which is chilled until set and then served with a raspberry and currant sauce.

Serves 4

1 tbsp powdered gelatine

450 g (1 lb) strawberries

25 g (scant 1 oz) caster sugar

500 g (1 lb 2 oz) plain low-fat bio yogurt

Raspberry and currant sauce

115 g (4 oz) red or black currants, plus a few
   extra on stalks to decorate

25 g (scant 1 oz) caster sugar

115 g (4 oz) raspberries

1 tbsp framboise (raspberry liqueur) or kirsch

Preparation and cooking time: 20 minutes, plus
   at least 2 hours chilling

1 Sprinkle the gelatine over 3 tbsp cold water in a small mixing bowl and leave to soak for 5 minutes or until spongy. Set the bowl over a pan of hot water and stir until the gelatine has dissolved. Remove from the heat and leave to cool.

2 Meanwhile, put the strawberries and sugar in a bowl and mash with a fork. Add the dissolved gelatine and then the yogurt, mixing well. Divide among 4 glasses or serving dishes of 200 ml (7 fl oz) capacity. Cover and chill for at least 2 hours or until set.

3 Meanwhile, make the sauce. Put the currants, sugar and 2 tsp water in a small saucepan and bring to the boil, stirring to dissolve the sugar. Simmer for 1 minute, then remove from the heat and add the raspberries. Purée in the pan with a hand-held blender, or crush with a fork, then press through a sieve.

4 Pour a little of the sauce over the top of each mousse and decorate with a stalk of currants. Serve the remaining sauce separately.

Another idea

● For a plum and yogurt bavarois, sprinkle 1 tbsp powdered gelatine over 3 tbsp apple juice and leave to soak for 5 minutes. Bring 200 ml (7 fl oz) semi-skimmed milk to boiling point. Meanwhile, whisk together 1 whole egg, 2 egg yolks, 1 tsp cornflour and 45 g (1½ oz) caster sugar in a bowl. Pour in the hot milk, whisking. Return the mixture to the rinsed-out pan and stir over a low heat for 3–4 minutes or until thickened. Remove from the heat and stir in the gelatine until dissolved. Pour the custard into a bowl and cool, stirring occasionally. Meanwhile, halve and stone 4 firm, ripe plums and put in a pan with 45 g (1½ oz) caster sugar and 170 ml (6 fl oz) apple juice. Poach for 8–10 minutes or until the plums are just soft. Remove them with a draining spoon. Simmer the poaching liquid for 5 minutes or until syrupy. Leave to cool. Stir 150 g (5½ oz) plain low-fat bio yogurt into the cooled custard, then fold in 150 ml (5 fl oz) lightly whipped whipping cream. Spoon a thin layer of the custard mixture into a chilled 1 litre (1¾ pint) ring mould, and arrange the cooled plums on top. Spoon in the remaining custard mixture. Chill for at least 2 hours or until set. Turn out and serve with the plum syrup.

Plus point

● Bio yogurts contain live bacteria that have a beneficial effect on the digestive system. These yogurts also have a milder, creamier flavour than normal yogurt.

Each serving provides

kcal 185, **protein** 11 g, **fat** 1 g (of which saturated fat 0.5 g), **carbohydrate** 33 g (of which sugars 33 g), **fibre** 3 g

✓✓✓	C
✓✓	calcium
✓	B₂, folate, niacin, copper, potassium, zinc

sweet finales

Pistachio floating islands

In this version of the classic French pudding, *îles flottantes*, fluffy poached meringues studded with pistachio nuts float on a creamy vanilla custard. A flourish of fresh blueberry coulis is the finishing touch.

Serves 4

Vanilla custard
600 ml (1 pint) semi-skimmed milk
1 vanilla pod
25 g (scant 1 oz) caster sugar
4 large egg yolks
1 tsp cornflour

Pistachio meringues
1 large egg white
45 g (1½ oz) caster sugar
30 g (1 oz) unsalted pistachio nuts, chopped

Blueberry coulis
250 g (8½ oz) blueberries
15 g (½ oz) icing sugar, sifted

Preparation and cooking time: about
   50 minutes, plus at least 30 minutes chilling

Each serving provides Ⓥ
kcal 283, **protein** 10 g, **fat** 12 g (of which saturated fat 4 g), **carbohydrate** 38 g (of which sugars 34 g), **fibre** 2 g

✓✓✓	B₁₂
✓✓	calcium
✓	A, B₁, B₂, C, folate, niacin, copper, iron, potassium, selenium, zinc

---

1 Pour the milk into a medium-sized frying pan. Split the vanilla pod down its length with a sharp knife and scrape out the tiny black seeds into the milk. Cut the pod in half and add to the pan with the sugar. Bring to a gentle simmer, stirring occasionally.

2 Meanwhile, in a clean bowl whisk the egg white for the meringues to soft peaks. Gradually whisk in the caster sugar, then continue whisking for about 1 minute or until the meringue is stiff and glossy. Gently fold in the pistachio nuts.

3 When the milk is just simmering, spoon on the meringue in 4 neat mounds. Poach gently for 5 minutes, turning once, until the meringues feel set. Remove with a draining spoon onto kitchen paper and set aside.

4 Strain the milk into a heavy-based saucepan. Mix together the egg yolks and cornflour, then whisk into the milk. Cook over a very low heat for 5–7 minutes, stirring all the time, until smooth and thickened. Do not allow the custard to boil or it will curdle. If it does start to curdle, immediately strain it through a fine sieve into a clean pan.

5 Remove the custard from the heat and pour it into a large, shallow serving bowl or onto 4 individual plates or dishes. Cover and chill for at least 30 minutes or up to 1 hour.

6 Meanwhile, make the blueberry coulis. Put the blueberries and icing sugar in a small saucepan with 2 tsp water. Simmer over a low heat, stirring occasionally, for 4–5 minutes or until the blueberries burst and release their juices. Press the mixture through a sieve and leave to cool.

7 Float the meringues on the custard and drizzle a little blueberry coulis over them. Serve immediately, with the rest of the coulis separately.

Plus points

● As long as eggs are not overcooked, there is no protein loss and they retain all their content of vitamins A, D and niacin. There can be some loss of vitamins B₁ and B₂, if eggs are cooked for a long time.

● Pistachios are a good source of vitamin B₁ and contain a small amount of carotene. Like other nuts, they are rich in potassium and low in sodium (unless salt is added during roasting).

● Blueberries, like all berries, are rich in vitamin C and also provide some beta-carotene. Both of these nutrients are important antioxidants.

sweet finales

Some more ideas

● Use frozen and thawed blueberries for the coulis.

● Omit the pistachios, if you prefer, or replace them with chopped pecan nuts.

● For lime and passion fruit floating islands, flavour the milk with the grated zest of 1 lime instead of vanilla. Make the meringues as in the main recipe, but without the pistachio nuts. Replace the blueberry coulis with a passion fruit coulis: halve 6 large, ripe passion fruits and scoop out the pulp into a small saucepan. Stir in 15 g (½ oz) caster sugar and cook over a low heat for 1–2 minutes, stirring, until the sugar has dissolved. Leave to cool.

Coffee junket

When you want a quickly made dessert, try this smooth and soothing Victorian favourite. It doesn't set firm but has the consistency of a wobbly jelly or crème caramel. As you need to take care not to overheat the milk, it's a good idea to use a thermometer to check the temperature accurately.

Serves 4

600 ml (1 pint) full-fat milk (not homogenised)

2 tbsp instant espresso coffee powder

1 tbsp caster sugar

1 tsp liquid rennet or 10 drops vegetarian rennet

To serve

15 g (½ oz) good dark chocolate (at least 70% cocoa solids), grated

2 bananas

4 tbsp single cream

Preparation time: 10 minutes, plus about 1–1½ hours setting and 2–3 hours chilling

1 Put the milk in a saucepan and stir in the espresso coffee and sugar. Heat the milk gently until it reaches 36°C (98°F), which is normal blood heat – the milk should feel just warm to the finger.

2 Pour the warm milk into a mixing bowl or jug and stir once or twice. Add the rennet and stir again. Pour into 4 shallow serving dishes. Set aside in a warm place and leave, undisturbed, for 1–1½ hours or until set. Then cover and chill for 2–3 hours.

3 To serve, sprinkle the grated chocolate over the top of each dessert. Slice the bananas, and serve the junket with the bananas and cream.

Some more ideas

- For vanilla junket, omit the coffee, and stir 1 tbsp pure vanilla extract into the warm milk after you have poured it into the bowl and before you add the rennet. Serve this with sliced mangoes.

- Try this easy milk pudding. Take 6 tbsp from 600 ml (1 pint) whole milk and mix it with 6 tbsp cornflour in a bowl to make a smooth paste. Heat the rest of the milk with 100 g (3½ oz) caster sugar in a heavy-based saucepan until the sugar has dissolved. Pour some of the hot milk into the cornflour mixture, stirring, then pour back into the pan. Heat, stirring constantly, until the mixture boils and starts to thicken, then simmer for 1 minute. Remove from the heat and stir in 2 tsp pure vanilla extract. Pour into a serving dish, cover the surface with cling film and leave to cool. Chill for at least 2 hours before serving with sliced bananas or peaches or mixed berries.

Plus points

- Using full-fat milk in this dessert gives it a delightful creaminess, yet it is healthily low in fat. Full-fat milk contains 3.9 g fat per 100 ml (3½ fl oz).

- Plain dark chocolate is a good source of copper, which amongst other functions helps the absorption of iron. This is useful, as dark chocolate is also a good source of iron.

Each serving provides

kcal 213, **protein** 6 g, **fat** 10 g (of which saturated fat 6 g), **carbohydrate** 27 g (of which sugars 26 g), **fibre** 1 g

✓✓	calcium
✓	A, B_2, B_6, B_{12}, potassium, zinc

Raspberry cranachan

This traditional Scottish dessert is quick and easy to put together, and the nutritious combination of cream, fromage frais, oatmeal and fresh fruit makes a superb sweet course for a special occasion meal. The whisky not only adds a taste of Scotland, but gives a fantastic kick to the flavour.

Serves 4

5 tbsp medium oatmeal

150 ml (5 fl oz) whipping cream

150 g (5½ oz) fromage frais

2 tbsp clear honey

2 tbsp whisky

400 g (14 oz) raspberries

Preparation time: about 20 minutes, plus
   15 minutes cooling

1 Preheat the grill to high. Line the rack in the grill pan with foil and spread the oatmeal over the foil. Toast under the grill for about 3 minutes, stirring once or twice, until the oatmeal is golden. Set aside to cool for about 15 minutes.

2 Put the cream and fromage frais in a bowl and whip together until thick. Stir in the honey and whisky, then fold in 4 tbsp of the toasted oatmeal.

3 Reserve a few raspberries for the decoration. Layer the remaining raspberries with the cream mixture in 4 glass serving dishes, starting with raspberries and ending with a layer of the cream mixture.

4 Decorate each dessert with a sprinkling of the remaining 1 tbsp toasted oatmeal and the reserved raspberries. Serve immediately (or keep in the fridge for up to 1 hour before serving).

Some more ideas

● Instead of raspberries, use other fresh fruit such as mixed berries, sliced peaches or nectarines, or a mixture of raspberries and peaches.

● Replace the whisky with brandy, or with orange or apple juice.

● Make a kiwi meringue crush. Whip 150 ml (5 fl oz) whipping cream. Lightly mash 150 g (5½ oz) cottage cheese to remove some of the larger lumps, then fold into the whipped cream, together with 1 tbsp light soft brown sugar, the finely grated zest of 1 small orange or 1 lime and 45 g (1½ oz) finely crumbled meringues. Layer the mixture in 4 glass dishes with 4 thinly sliced kiwi fruit. Decorate with 15 g (½ oz) toasted flaked almonds.

Plus points

● A pudding such as this is usually made with double cream. Whipping cream is lower in fat and calories than double cream and mixing the cream with fromage frais reduces the fat content even further.

● Since ancient times honey has been used as a food, a sweetener and a preservative. Honey is sweeter than sugar due to its fructose content, and it is lower in calories on a weight for weight basis because it has a higher water content.

Each serving provides Ⓥ

kcal 317, **protein** 7 g, **fat** 20 g (of which saturated fat 11 g), **carbohydrate** 26 g (of which sugars 14 g), **fibre** 4 g

✓✓	A, C
✓	B₁, B₂, B₁₂, E, folate, calcium, copper, iron, zinc

sweet finales

Blackberry ripple frozen yogurt

Blackberries rarely make an appearance in commercial ice creams, so all the more reason to use them for a home-made frozen dessert. This creamy custard-based ice cream is lightened with Greek-style yogurt and flavoured with a hint of orange, and a fresh blackberry purée is stirred through for a pretty purple ripple effect.

Serves 4

300 ml (10 fl oz) full-fat milk

finely grated zest of 1 orange

1 large egg

2 large egg yolks

55 g (2 oz) caster sugar

1 tsp cornflour

1 tsp pure vanilla extract

250 g (8½ oz) Greek-style yogurt

125 g (4½ oz) blackberries to decorate

Blackberry purée

115 g (4 oz) blackberries

30 g (1 oz) caster sugar

Preparation time: about 35 minutes, plus cooling and freezing

Each serving provides Ⓥ

kcal 276, protein 9 g, fat 12.5 g (of which saturated fat 6 g), carbohydrate 34 g (of which sugars 32 g), fibre 2 g

✓✓✓	B$_{12}$
✓✓	A, calcium
✓	B$_2$, C, E, folate, niacin, copper, potassium, zinc

1 Warm the milk in a heavy-based saucepan with the orange zest until scalding hot. Meanwhile, put the whole egg, egg yolks, sugar, cornflour and vanilla extract in a mixing bowl, and whisk together until pale and creamy.

2 Stir the milk into the egg mixture, then return to the pan and cook over a low heat, stirring constantly, until thickened. Do not allow the custard to boil. Remove from the heat and set aside to cool.

3 When the custard is cold, beat in the yogurt. Pour the mixture into an ice-cream machine and churn according to the manufacturer's instructions until the mixture is thick and slushy.

4 Alternatively, pour the mixture into a freezerproof container and freeze for 2 hours or until beginning to set around the edges. Tip out into a bowl and whisk well with a balloon whisk or electric mixer to break down the ice crystals, then return to the container. Freeze for a further 1½ hours.

5 Meanwhile, make the purée. Put the blackberries in a saucepan with the sugar and 1 tbsp water. Heat until the berries are soft and juicy, then bring to the boil and boil for 1–2 minutes to reduce slightly. Remove from the heat and cool. Press the blackberries through a nylon sieve to make a smooth purée.

6 If using an ice-cream machine, transfer the frozen yogurt to a rigid plastic container, then lightly stir in the blackberry purée to make a ripple effect. If frozen in a container, tip out into a bowl and whisk well until softened, then swirl in the blackberry purée and return to the container. Freeze for a further 3 hours, or overnight, until firm. (The frozen yogurt can be kept, covered, in the freezer for 3 months.)

7 About 45 minutes before serving, remove the frozen yogurt from the freezer so it can soften a little. Scoop into glasses and decorate with berries.

Plus points

• Blackberries are not only an excellent source of vitamin C, they are also one of the richest fruit sources of vitamin E.

• This delicious frozen yogurt is much lower in sugar and calories than most commercial frozen yogurts.

Some more ideas

● Make blueberry ripple frozen yogurt, using fresh or frozen and thawed blueberries instead of blackberries.

● Instead of vanilla extract, add 1 tsp ground cinnamon to the egg mixture in step 1.

● For strawberry frozen yogurt, make the custard as in the main recipe, but omit the vanilla extract. Cool, then add the yogurt. Gently cook 500 g (1 lb 2 oz) strawberries with the juice of ½ lemon and 55 g (2 oz) caster sugar until soft. Leave to cool, then press through a sieve. Beat the strawberry purée evenly into the custard and yogurt mixture, then freeze as in the main recipe.

A glossary of nutritional terms

Antioxidants These are compounds that help to protect the body's cells against the damaging effects of free radicals. Vitamins C and E, beta-carotene (the plant form of vitamin A) and the mineral selenium, together with many of the phytochemicals found in fruit and vegetables, all act as antioxidants.

Calorie A unit used to measure the energy value of food and the intake and use of energy by the body. The scientific definition of 1 calorie is the amount of heat required to raise the temperature of 1 gram of water by 1 degree Centigrade. This is such a small amount that in this country we tend to use the term kilocalories (abbreviated to *kcal*), which is equivalent to 1000 calories. Energy values can also be measured in kilojoules (kJ): 1 kcal = 4.2 kJ.

A person's energy (calorie) requirement varies depending on his or her age, sex and level of activity. The estimated average daily energy requirements are:

Age (years)	Female (kcal)	Male (kcal)
1–3	1165	1230
4–6	1545	1715
7–10	1740	1970
11–14	1845	2220
15–18	2110	2755
19–49	1940	2550
50–59	1900	2550
60–64	1900	2380
65–74	1900	2330

Carbohydrates These energy-providing substances are present in varying amounts in different foods and are found in three main forms: sugars, starches and non-starch polysaccharides (NSP), usually called fibre.

There are two types of sugars: *intrinsic sugars*, which occur naturally in fruit (fructose) and sweet-tasting vegetables, and *extrinsic sugars*, which include lactose (from milk) and all the non-milk extrinsic sugars (NMEs) – sucrose (table sugar), honey, treacle, molasses and so on. The NMEs, or 'added' sugars, provide only calories, whereas foods containing intrinsic sugars also offer vitamins, minerals and fibre. Added sugars (*simple carbohydrates*) are digested and absorbed rapidly to provide energy very quickly. Starches and fibre (*complex carbohydrates*), on the other hand, break down more slowly to offer a longer-term energy source (see also Glycaemic Index). Starchy carbohydrates are found in bread, pasta, rice,

wholegrain and breakfast cereals, and potatoes and other starchy vegetables such as parsnips, sweet potatoes and yams.

Healthy eating guidelines recommend that at least half of our daily energy (calories) should come from carbohydrates, and that most of this should be from complex carbohydrates. No more than 11% of our total calorie intake should come from 'added' sugars. For an average woman aged 19–49 years, this would mean a total carbohydrate intake of 259 g per day, of which 202 g should be from starch and intrinsic sugars and no more than 57 from added sugars. For a man of the same age, total carbohydrates each day should be about 340 g (265 g from starch and intrinsic sugars and 75 g from added sugars).

See also Fibre and Glycogen.

Cholesterol There are two types of cholesterol – the soft waxy substance called blood cholesterol, which is an integral part of human cell membranes, and dietary cholesterol, which is contained in food. *Blood cholesterol* is important in the formation of some hormones and it aids digestion. High blood cholesterol levels are known to be an important risk factor for coronary heart disease, but most of the cholesterol in our blood is made by the liver – only about 25% comes from cholesterol in food. So while it would seem that the amount of cholesterol-rich foods in the diet would have a direct effect on blood cholesterol levels, in fact the best way to reduce blood cholesterol is to eat less saturated fat and to increase intake of foods containing soluble fibre.

Fat Although a small amount of fat is essential for good health, most people consume far too much. Healthy eating guidelines recommend that no more than 33% of our daily energy intake (calories) should come from fat. Each gram of fat contains 9 kcal, more than twice as many calories as carbohydrate or protein, so for a woman aged 19–49 years this means a daily maximum of 71 g fat, and for a man in the same age range 93.5 g fat.

Fats can be divided into 3 main groups: saturated, monounsaturated and polyunsaturated, depending on the chemical structure of the fatty acids they contain. *Saturated fatty acids* are found mainly in animal fats such as butter and other dairy products and in fatty meat. A high intake of saturated fat is known to be a risk factor for coronary heart disease and certain types of cancer. Current guidelines are that no more than 10% of our daily calories should come from saturated fats, which is about 21.5 g for an adult woman and 28.5 g for a man.

Where saturated fats tend to be solid at room temperature, the *unsaturated fatty acids* –

monounsaturated and polyunsaturated – tend to be liquid. *Monounsaturated fats* are found predominantly in olive oil, groundnut (peanut) oil, rapeseed oil and avocados. Foods high in *polyunsaturates* include most vegetable oils – the exceptions are palm oil and coconut oil, both of which are saturated.

Both saturated and monounsaturated fatty acids can be made by the body, but certain polyunsaturated fatty acids – known as *essential fatty acids* – must be supplied by food. There are 2 'families' of these essential fatty acids: *omega-6*, derived from linoleic acid, and *omega-3*, from linolenic acid. The main food sources of the omega-6 family are vegetable oils such as olive and sunflower; omega-3 fatty acids are provided by oily fish, nuts, and vegetable oils such as soya and rapeseed.

When vegetable oils are hydrogenated (hardened) to make margarine and reduced-fat spreads, their unsaturated fatty acids can be changed into trans fatty acids, or '*trans fats*'. These artificially produced trans fats are believed to act in the same way as saturated fats within the body – with the same risks to health. Current healthy eating guidelines suggest that no more than 2% of our daily calories should come from trans fats, which is about 4.3 g for an adult woman and 5.6 g for a man. In thinking about the amount of trans fats you consume, remember that major sources are processed foods such as biscuits, pies, cakes and crisps.

Fibre Technically non-starch polysaccharides (NSP), fibre is the term commonly used to describe several different compounds, such as pectin, hemicellulose, lignin and gums, which are found in the cell walls of all plants. The body cannot digest fibre, nor does it have much nutritional value, but it plays an important role in helping us to stay healthy.

Fibre can be divided into 2 groups – soluble and insoluble. Both types are provided by most plant foods, but some foods are particularly good sources of one type or the other. *Soluble fibre* (in oats, pulses, fruit and vegetables) can help to reduce high blood cholesterol levels and to control blood sugar levels by slowing down the absorption of sugar. *Insoluble fibre* (in wholegrain cereals, pulses, fruit and vegetables) increases stool bulk and speeds the passage of waste material through the body. In this way it helps to prevent constipation, haemorrhoids and diverticular disease, and may protect against bowel cancer.

Our current intake of fibre is around 12 g a day. Healthy eating guidelines suggest that we need to increase this amount to 18 g a day.

Free radicals These highly reactive molecules can cause damage to cell walls and DNA (the genetic material found within cells). They are believed to be involved in the development of heart disease, some cancers and premature ageing. Free radicals are produced naturally by

glossary

156

the body in the course of everyday life, but certain factors, such as cigarette smoke, pollution and over-exposure to sunlight, can accelerate their production.

Gluten A protein found in wheat and, to a lesser degree, in rye, barley and oats, but not in corn (maize) or rice. People with *coeliac disease* have a sensitivity to gluten and need to eliminate all gluten-containing foods, such as bread, pasta, cakes and biscuits, from their diet.

Glycaemic Index (GI) This is used to measure the rate at which carbohydrate foods are digested and converted into sugar (glucose) to raise blood sugar levels and provide energy. Foods with a high GI are quickly broken down and offer an immediate energy fix, while those with a lower GI are absorbed more slowly, making you feel full for longer and helping to keep blood sugar levels constant. High-GI foods include table sugar, honey, mashed potatoes and watermelon. Low-GI foods include pulses, wholewheat cereals, apples, cherries, dried apricots, pasta and oats.

Glycogen This is one of the 2 forms in which energy from carbohydrates is made available for use by the body (the other is *glucose*). Whereas glucose is converted quickly from carbohydrates and made available in the blood for a fast energy fix, glycogen is stored in the liver and muscles to fuel longer-term energy needs. When the body has used up its immediate supply of glucose, the stored glycogen is broken down into glucose to continue supplying energy.

Minerals These inorganic substances perform a wide range of vital functions in the body. The *macrominerals* – calcium, chloride, magnesium, potassium, phosphorus and sodium – are needed in relatively large quantities, whereas much smaller amounts are required of the remainder, called *microminerals*. Some microminerals (selenium, magnesium and iodine, for example) are needed in such tiny amounts that they are known as *'trace elements'*.

There are important differences in the body's ability to absorb minerals from different foods, and this can be affected by the presence of other substances. For example, oxalic acid, present in spinach, interferes with the absorption of much of the iron and calcium spinach contains.
• *Calcium* is essential for the development of strong bones and teeth. It also plays an important role in blood clotting. Good sources include dairy products, canned fish (eaten with their bones) and dark green, leafy vegetables.
• *Chloride* helps to maintain the body's fluid balance. The main source in the diet is table salt.
• *Chromium* is important in the regulation of blood sugar levels, as well as levels of fat and cholesterol in the blood. Good dietary sources include red meat, liver, eggs, seafood, cheese and wholegrain cereals.

• *Copper*, component of many enzymes, is needed for bone growth and the formation of connective tissue. It helps the body to absorb iron from food. Good sources include offal, shellfish, mushrooms, cocoa, nuts and seeds.
• *Iodine* is an important component of the thyroid hormones, which govern the rate and efficiency at which food is converted into energy. Good sources include seafood, seaweed and vegetables (depending on the iodine content of the soil in which they are grown).
• *Iron* is an essential component of haemoglobin, the pigment in red blood cells that carries oxygen around the body. Good sources are offal, red meat, dried apricots and prunes, and iron-fortified breakfast cereals.
• *Magnesium* is important for healthy bones, the release of energy from food, and nerve and muscle function. Good sources include wholegrain cereals, peas and other green vegetables, pulses, dried fruit and nuts.
• *Manganese* is a vital component of several enzymes that are involved in energy production and many other functions. Good dietary sources include nuts, cereals, brown rice, pulses and wholemeal bread.
• *Molybdenum* is an essential component of several enzymes, including those involved in the production of DNA. Good sources are offal, yeast, pulses, wholegrain cereals and green leafy vegetables.
• *Phosphorus* is important for healthy bones and teeth and for the release of energy from foods. It is found in most foods. Particularly good sources include dairy products, red meat, poultry, fish and eggs.
• *Potassium*, along with sodium, is important in maintaining fluid balance and regulating blood pressure, and is essential for the transmission of nerve impulses. Good sources include fruit, especially bananas and citrus fruits, nuts, seeds, potatoes and pulses.
• *Selenium* is a powerful antioxidant that protects cells against damage by free radicals. Good dietary sources are meat, fish, dairy foods, brazil nuts, avocados and lentils.
• *Sodium* works with potassium to regulate fluid balance, and is essential for nerve and muscle function. Only a little sodium is needed – we tend to get too much in our diet. The main source in the diet is table salt, as well as salty processed foods and ready-prepared foods.
• *Sulphur* is a component of 2 essential amino acids. Protein foods are the main source.
• *Zinc* is vital for normal growth, as well as reproduction and immunity. Good dietary sources include oysters, red meat, peanuts and sunflower seeds.

Phytochemicals These biologically active compounds, found in most plant foods, are believed to be beneficial in disease prevention. There are literally thousands of different phytochemicals, amongst which are the following:

• *Allicin*, a phytochemical found in garlic, onions, leeks, chives and shallots, is believed to help lower high blood cholesterol levels and stimulate the immune system.
• *Bioflavonoids*, of which there are at least 6000, are found mainly in fruit and sweet-tasting vegetables. Different bioflavonoids have different roles – some are antioxidants, while others act as anti-disease agents. A sub-group of these phytochemicals, called *flavonols*, includes the antioxidant *quercetin*, which is believed to reduce the risk of heart disease and help to protect against cataracts. Quercetin is found in tea, red wine, grapes and broad beans.
• *Carotenoids*, the best known of which are *beta-carotene* and *lycopene*, are powerful antioxidants thought to help protect us against certain types of cancer. Highly coloured fruits and vegetables, such as blackcurrants, mangoes, tomatoes, carrots, sweet potatoes, pumpkin and dark green, leafy vegetables, are excellent sources of carotenoids.
• *Coumarins* are believed to help protect against cancer by inhibiting the formation of tumours. Oranges are a rich source.
• *Glucosinolates*, found mainly in cruciferous vegetables, particularly broccoli, Brussels sprouts, cabbage, kale and cauliflower, are believed to have strong anti-cancer effects. *Sulphoraphane* is one of the powerful cancer-fighting substances produced by glucosinolates.
• *Phytoestrogens* have a chemical structure similar to the female hormone oestrogen, and they are believed to help protect against hormone-related cancers such as breast and prostate cancer. One of the types of these phytochemicals, called *isoflavones*, may also help to relieve symptoms associated with the menopause. Soya beans and chickpeas are a particularly rich source of isoflavones.

Protein This nutrient, necessary for growth and development, for maintenance and repair of cells, and for the production of enzymes, antibodies and hormones, is essential to keep the body working efficiently. Protein is made up of *amino acids*, which are compounds containing the 4 elements that are necessary for life: carbon, hydrogen, oxygen and nitrogen. We need all of the 20 amino acids commonly found in plant and animal proteins. The human body can make 12 of these, but the remaining 8 – called *essential amino acids* – must be obtained from the food we eat.

Protein comes in a wide variety of foods. Meat, fish, dairy products, eggs and soya beans contain all of the essential amino acids, and are therefore called first-class protein foods. Pulses, nuts, seeds and cereals are also good sources of protein, but do not contain the full range of essential amino acids. In practical terms, this really doesn't matter – as long as you include a variety of different protein foods in your diet, your body will get all the amino acids it needs. It is important, though, to eat protein foods

glossary

every day because the essential amino acids cannot be stored in the body for later use.

The RNI of protein for women aged 19–49 years is 45 g per day and for men of the same age 55 g. In the UK most people eat more protein than they need, although this isn't normally a problem.

Reference Nutrient Intake (RNI) This denotes the average daily amount of vitamins and minerals thought to be sufficient to meet the nutritional needs of almost all individuals within the population. The figures, published by the Department of Health, vary depending on age, sex and specific nutritional needs such as pregnancy. RNIs are equivalent to what used to be called Recommended Daily Amounts or Allowances (RDA).

RNIs for adults (19–49 years)

Vitamin A	600–700 mcg
Vitamin B_1	0.8 mg for women, 1 mg for men
Vitamin B_2	1.1 mg for women, 1.3 mg for men
Niacin	13 mg for women, 17 mg for men
Vitamin B_6	1.2 mg for women, 1.4 mg for men
Vitamin B_{12}	1.5 mg
Folate	200 mcg (400 mcg for first trimester of pregnancy)
Vitamin C	40 mg
Vitamin E	no recommendation in the UK; the EC RDA is 10 mg, which has been used in all recipe analyses in this book
Calcium	700 mg
Chloride	2500 mg
Copper	1.2 mg
Iodine	140 mcg
Iron	14.8 mg for women, 8.7 mg for men
Magnesium	270–300 mg
Phosphorus	550 mg
Potassium	3500 mg
Selenium	60 mcg for women, 75 mcg for men
Sodium	1600 mg
Zinc	7 mg for women, 9.5 mg for men

Vitamins These are organic compounds that are essential for good health. Although they are required in only small amounts, each one has specific vital functions to perform. Most vitamins cannot be made by the human body, and therefore must be obtained from the diet. The body is capable of storing some vitamins (A, D, E, K and B_{12}), but the rest need to be provided by the diet on a regular basis. A well-balanced diet, containing a wide variety of different foods, is the best way to ensure that you get all the vitamins you need.

Vitamins can be divided into 2 groups: *water-soluble* (B complex and C) and *fat-soluble* (A, D, E and K). Water-soluble vitamins are easily destroyed during processing, storage, and the preparation and cooking of food. The fat-soluble vitamins are less vulnerable to losses during cooking and processing.

• *Vitamin A* (retinol) is essential for healthy vision, eyes, skin and growth. Good sources include dairy products, offal (especially liver), eggs and oily fish. Vitamin A can also be obtained from *beta-carotene*, the pigment found in highly coloured fruit and vegetables. In addition to acting as a source of vitamin A, beta-carotene has an important role to play as an antioxidant in its own right.

• *The B Complex vitamins* have very similar roles to play in nutrition, and many of them occur together in the same foods.

Vitamin B_1 (thiamin) is essential in the release of energy from carbohydrates. Good sources include milk, offal, meat (especially pork), wholegrain and fortified breakfast cereals, nuts and pulses, yeast extract and wheat germ. White flour and bread are fortified with B_1 in the UK.

Vitamin B_2 (riboflavin) is vital for growth, healthy skin and eyes, and the release of energy from food. Good sources include milk, meat, offal, eggs, cheese, fortified breakfast cereals, yeast extract and green leafy vegetables.

Niacin (nicotinic acid), sometimes called vitamin B_3, plays an important role in the release of energy within the cells. Unlike the other B vitamins it can be made by the body from the essential amino acid tryptophan. Good sources include meat, offal, fish, fortified breakfast cereals and pulses. White flour and bread are fortified with niacin in the UK.

Pantothenic acid, sometimes called vitamin B_5, is involved in a number of metabolic reactions, including energy production. This vitamin is present in most foods; notable exceptions are fat, oil and sugar. Good sources include liver, kidneys, yeast, egg yolks, fish roe, wheat germ, nuts, pulses and fresh vegetables.

Vitamin B_6 (pyridoxine) helps the body to utilise protein and contributes to the formation of haemoglobin for red blood cells. B_6 is found in a wide range of foods including meat, liver, fish, eggs, wholegrain cereals, some vegetables, pulses, brown rice, nuts and yeast extract.

Vitamin B_{12} (cyanocobalamin) is vital for growth, the formation of red blood cells and maintenance of a healthy nervous system. B_{12} is unique in that it is principally found in foods of animal origin. Vegetarians who eat dairy products will get enough, but vegans need to ensure they include food fortified with B_{12} in their diet. Good sources of B_{12} include liver, kidneys, oily fish, meat, cheese, eggs and milk.

Folate (folic acid) is involved in the manufacture of amino acids and in the production of red blood cells. Recent research suggests that folate may also help to protect against heart disease. Good sources of folate are green leafy vegetables, liver, pulses, eggs, wholegrain cereal products and fortified breakfast cereals, brewers' yeast, wheatgerm, nuts and fruit, especially grapefruit and oranges.

Biotin is needed for various metabolic reactions and the release of energy from foods. Good sources include liver, oily fish, brewers' yeast, kidneys, egg yolks and brown rice.

• *Vitamin C* (ascorbic acid) is essential for growth and vital for the formation of collagen (a protein needed for healthy bones, teeth, gums, blood capillaries and all connective tissue). It plays an important role in the healing of wounds and fractures, and acts as a powerful antioxidant. Vitamin C is found mainly in fruit and vegetables.

• *Vitamin D* (cholecalciferol) is essential for growth and the absorption of calcium, and thus for the formation of healthy bones. It is also involved in maintaining a healthy nervous system. The amount of vitamin D occurring naturally in foods is small, and it is found in very few foods – good sources are oily fish (and fish liver oil supplements), eggs and liver, as well as breakfast cereals, margarine and full-fat milk that are fortified with vitamin D. Most vitamin D, however, does not come from the diet but is made by the body when the skin is exposed to sunlight.

• *Vitamin E* is not one vitamin, but a number of related compounds called tocopherols that function as antioxidants. Good sources of vitamin E are vegetable oils, polyunsaturated margarines, wheatgerm, sunflower seeds, nuts, oily fish, eggs, wholegrain cereals, avocados and spinach.

• *Vitamin K* is essential for the production of several proteins, including prothrombin which is involved in the clotting of blood. It has been found to exist in 3 forms, one of which is obtained from food while the other 2 are made by the bacteria in the intestine. Vitamin K_1, which is the form found in food, is present in broccoli, cabbage, spinach, milk, margarine, vegetable oils, particularly soya oil, cereals, liver, alfalfa and kelp.

Nutritional analyses

The nutritional analysis of each recipe has been carried out using data from *The Composition of Foods* with additional data from food manufacturers where appropriate. Because the level and availability of different nutrients can vary, depending on factors like growing conditions and breed of animal, the figures are intended as an approximate guide only.

The analyses include vitamins A, B_1, B_2, B_6, B_{12}, niacin, folate, C, D and E, and the minerals calcium, copper, iron, potassium, selenium and zinc. Other vitamins and minerals are not included, as deficiencies are rare. Optional ingredients and optional serving suggestions have not been included in the calculations.

glossary

Index

Printing and binding: Tien Wah Press Limited, Singapore
Separations: Colour Systems Ltd, London
Paper: StoraEnso

Book code: 400-199-01
ISBN: 0 276 42890 0
Oracle Code: 250008439S